T0212982

Lecture Notes in Artificial Intelligence   10685

Subseries of Lecture Notes in Computer Science

LNAI Series Editors

Randy Goebel
University of Alberta, Edmonton, Canada
Yuzuru Tanaka
Hokkaido University, Sapporo, Japan
Wolfgang Wahlster
DFKI and Saarland University, Saarbrücken, Germany

LNAI Founding Series Editor

Joerg Siekmann
DFKI and Saarland University, Saarbrücken, Germany

More information about this series at http://www.springer.com/series/1244

Sara Montagna · Pedro Henriques Abreu
Sylvain Giroux · Michael Ignaz Schumacher (Eds.)

Agents and Multi-Agent Systems for Health Care

10th International Workshop, A2HC 2017
São Paulo, Brazil, May 8, 2017
and International Workshop, A-HEALTH 2017
Porto, Portugal, June 21, 2017
Revised and Extended Selected Papers

 Springer

Editors
Sara Montagna (iD)
University of Bologna
Cesena
Italy

Pedro Henriques Abreu (iD)
University of Coimbra
Coimbra
Portugal

Sylvain Giroux (iD)
Université de Sherbrooke
Sherbrooke, QC
Canada

Michael Ignaz Schumacher (iD)
University of Applied Sciences of Western
   Switzerland
Delémont
Switzerland

ISSN 0302-9743   ISSN 1611-3349   (electronic)
Lecture Notes in Artificial Intelligence
ISBN 978-3-319-70886-7   ISBN 978-3-319-70887-4   (eBook)
https://doi.org/10.1007/978-3-319-70887-4

Library of Congress Control Number: 2017959621

LNCS Sublibrary: SL7 – Artificial Intelligence

Printed on acid-free paper

This Springer imprint is published by Springer Nature
The registered company is Springer International Publishing AG
The registered company address is: Gewerbestrasse 11, 6330 Cham, Switzerland

Preface

Intelligent agent-based systems constitute one of the most exciting research areas in artificial intelligence. Owing to the growing interest in the application of agent-based systems in health care, a number of applications addressing clinical problems are already based on agent technology. Current topics of research include personalized health systems for remote and autonomous tele-assistance, communication, and co-operation between distributed intelligent agents to manage patient care, information agents that retrieve medical information from distributed repositories, intelligent and distributed data mining, and multi-agent systems that assist the doctors in the tasks of monitoring, decision support, and diagnosis. Several methodological and technical problems have been discovered by researchers who attempt to deploy agent-based systems in the medical area; just to name a few, the growing number of huge databases that need to be integrated (e.g., genetic data from next-generation sequencing), the difficulty to integrate new agent-based systems with legacy software, the need to apply changing national and international laws and regulations concerning the privacy of medical data, and the security of the transaction of patient information between agents. In 2017, these topics were discussed in two major workshops:

1. The 10th edition of the Workshop on Agents Applied in Health Care (A2HC 2017) hosted at AAMAS 2017, the 16th International Conference on Autonomous Agents and Multiagent Systems, which took place in São Paulo, Brazil on May 8, 2017
2. Workshop on Agents and Multi-agent Systems for AAL and e-Health (A-HEALTH 2017) hosted at PAAMS 2017, the 15th International Conference on Practical Applications of Agents and Multi-Agent Systems, which took place in Porto, Portugal, during June 21, 2017

For the 2017 edition of the two workshops, we received a total of 16 submissions, from which we selected nine for presentation (near 55% acceptance). This proceedings joint volume gathers peer-reviewed extended versions of selected papers presented at these workshops.

We are deeply grateful to all the participants for their lively contribution during the presentation of the papers and during the general discussion about the challenges that the application of agent technology in the health-care field faces. We are also very grateful to all the members of the Program Committee for their hard work. A special thanks goes to Juan Antonio Rodríguez Aguilar (IIIA-CSIC, Spain) and Gita Sukthankar (University of Central Florida, USA) for their work as AAMAS 2017 workshop chairs. Finally, a sincere thanks to the co-organizers of the workshops: Márcia Ito for managing the local organization of A2HC, Daniel Castro Silvia for his valuable work in the review phase, Eloisa Vargiu and Kasper Hallenborg for supporting us in various phases of the workshop organization.

November 2017   Sara Montagna
                                                    Pedro Henriques Abreu
                                                            Sylvain Giroux
                                                   Michael Ignaz Schumacher

A2HC 2017 Organization

Organizing Committee

Daniel Castro Silva	University of Porto, Portugal
Pedro Henriques Abreu	University of Coimbra, Portugal
Márcia Ito	IBM Brazil/University of Technology of São Paulo, Brazil
Sara Montagna	University of Bologna, Italy
Michael Schumacher	University of Applied Sciences and Arts Western Switzerland (HES-SO), Sierre, Switzerland
Eloisa Vargiu	Fundació Eurecat - eHealth Unit, Spain

Program Committee

Agostino Poggi	University of Parma, Italy
Aldo Franco Dragoni	Marche Polytechnic University, Italy
Andrea Omicini	University of Bologna, Italy
Antonio Moreno	Universitat Rovira i Virgili, Tarragona, Spain
Beatriz López Ibáñez	University of Girona, Spain
David Isern	Universitat Rovira i Virgili, Spain
Davide Calvaresi	Scuola Superiore Sant'Anna, Pisa, Italy
Diana Adamatti	Universidade Federal do Rio Grande, Brazil
Filipe Portela	Univerity of Minho, Portugal
Francisco Grimaldo	University of Valencia, Spain
Juan Carlos Nieves	Universitat Umea, Sweden
Kasper Hallenborg	University of Southern Denmark, Denmark
Lenka Lhotska	Czech Technical University, Czech Republic
Luiz Cysneiros	York University, Canada
Marcelo Ladeira	Universidade de Brasília, Brazil
Martin Beer	Sheffield Hallam University, UK
Szymon Wilk	Poznan University of Technology, Poland
Vassilis Koutkias	Aristotle University of Thessaloniki, Greece
Visara Urovi	University of Maastricht, The Netherlands
Viviana Mascardi	University of Genoa, Italy

A-HEALTH 2017 Organization

Organizing Committee

Kasper Hallenborg   University of Southern Denmark, Denmark
Sylvain Giroux   University of Sherbrooke, Canada

Program Committee

Juan M. Corchado   University of Salamanca, Spain
Javier Bajo   Technical University of Madrid, Spain
Juan F. De Paz   University of Salamanca, Spain
Sara Rodríguez   University of Salamanca, Spain
Valerie Camps   Paul Sabatier University of Toulouse, France
Cristian I. Pinzón   Technical University of Panama, Panama
Sigeru Omatu   Osaka Institute of Technology, Japan
Paulo Novais   University of Minho, Portugal
Luis F. Castillo   University of Caldas, Colombia
Florentino Fernandez   University of Vigo, Spain
Belén Pérez Lancho   University of Salamanca, Spain
Jesús García Herrero   Carlos III University of Madrid, Spain
Helena Lindgren   University of Umea, Sweden
Goretti Marrciros   Instituto Superior de Engenharia do Porto, Portugal
Gaetano Carmelo   University of Catania, Italy
La Delfa Tiancheng Li   Northwestern Polytechnical University, China

Contents

Teleassistance, Remote and Monitoring Agents Applications

Agent-Based Systems for Telerehabilitation: Strengths, Limitations and Future Challenges

Davide Calvaresi[1,2](✉) ⓘ, Michael Schumacher[2] ⓘ, Mauro Marinoni[1] ⓘ,
Roger Hilfiker[3] ⓘ, Aldo F. Dragoni[3] ⓘ, and Giorgio Buttazzo[1] ⓘ

[1] Scuola Superiore Sant'Anna, Pisa, Italy
{d.calvaresi,m.marinoni,g.buttazzo}@sssup.it
[2] University of Applied Sciences Western Switzerland, Sierre, Switzerland
michael.schumacher@hevs.ch
[3] Università Politecnica delle Marche, Ancona, Italy
roger.hilfiker@hevs.ch, a.f.dragoni@univpm.it

Abstract. Telerehabilitation in older adults is most needed in the
patient environments, rather than in formal ambulatories or hospitals.
Supporting such practices brings significant advantages to patients, their
family, formal and informal caregivers, clinicians, and researchers. Several techniques and technologies have been developed aiming at facilitating and enhancing the effectiveness of telerehabilitation. This paper gives
a quick overview of the state of the art, investigating video-based, wearable, robotic, distributed, and gamified telerehabilitation solutions. In
particular, agent-based solutions are analyzed and discussed addressing
strength, limitations, and future challenges. Elaborating on functional
requirements expressed by professional physiotherapists and researchers,
the need for extending multi-agent systems (MAS) peculiarities at the
sensing level in wearable solutions establishes new research challenges.
Employed in cyber-physical scenarios with users-sensors and sensors-
sensors interactions, MAS are requested to handle timing constraints,
scarcity of resources and new communication means, which are crucial
for providing real-time feedback and coaching.

Keywords: Multi-agent systems · Wearable multi-agent systems
Real-time multi-agent systems · Telerehabilitation · Real-time systems
Review · MAS

1 Introduction

Healthcare institutions are facing the strain of a significantly larger elderly population [1]. Lengthening life expectancy is met by an increasing demand for medical and technological contributions to extend the "good-health", and disability-
free period.

The major factor catalyzing the elderly's impairing process is the progres-
sive reduction of mobility, due to the natural aging process, inactivity, diseases such as osteoarthritis, stroke or other neurological conditions, falls with

S. Montagna et al. (Eds.): A2HC 2017/A-HEALTH 2017, LNAI 10685, pp. 3–24, 2017.
https://doi.org/10.1007/978-3-319-70887-4_1

4 D. Calvaresi et al.

its consequences, such as fear of falls (leading to inactivity), or fractures (needing surgery). Despite the emergence of less-invasive surgical techniques, postintervention rehabilitation still requires extended periods and tailored therapies, which usually involve complications. Performing traditional rehabilitative practices is leading to a significant increase in public-health costs and, in some cases, a lack of resources, thus worsening the services' quality. Rehabilitation is often a long process and needs to be sustained long after the end of the acute care. Simplifying the access to health services [2] can raise the number of patients, maintaining (or even increasing) the quality of care. For example, patients requiring support, such as continuous or selective monitoring, can benefit from systems that automatically transmit the information gathered in their domestic environment to the health clinics, thus enabling telemonitoring on their health conditions [3]. Although in traditional solutions telemonitoring is a self-contained practice limited to passively observing the patients, the need for remote sensing is crucially coupled with the need for coaching older adults in their daily living [4,5].

For example, a critical activity such as telerehabilitation cannot be limited to observing the patients' behaviors. Indeed, patient adherence and acceptability of rehabilitative practices need to be actively enhanced, overcoming pitfalls due to motor (e.g., endurance), non-motor (e.g., fatigue, pain, dysautonomic symptoms, and motivational), and cognitive deficits. According to Rodriguez et al. [6], telerehabilitation can be formally defined as:

"the application of telecommunication, remote sensing and operation technologies, and computing technologies to assist with the provision of medical rehabilitation services at a distance."

Patients, physiotherapists, and health institutes can gain several benefits from an extensive adoption of telerehabilitation systems [7]. Considering the economical point of view, Mozaffarian et al. [8] figured out that the total cost of stroke in the US was estimable to be 34.3 billion dollars in 2008, rising up to 69.1 billion dollars in 2016.

Even though to date they are not precisely quantifiable due to insufficient evidence [9], Mutingi et al. [10] presented as *"inevitable advantages"* (i) a substantial cost saving primarily due to the reduction of specialized human resources, (ii) an enhancement of patient comfort and lifestyle, and (iii) improvements of therapy and decision making processes. Moreover, Morreale et al. [11] mentioned one of the most appreciated benefits: the increase of adherence to rehabilitation protocols.

The multitude of scientific contributions fostering telerehabilitation exploits new technologies and various architectures to better understand and serve user requirements. However, due to technological or technical limitations, physiotherapists' needs have not yet been completely satisfied. To fill this gap, a system evolution is required. For example, telerehabilitation systems cannot offer the same behavior to users with diverse conditions. Viceversa, according to the environment condition, they must rather be able to adapt themselves to the user needs [6].

Telerehabilitation is characterized by a very delicate equilibrium between environment, devices, and users. Thus, the capabilities such as self-adaptation, flexibility, and ubiquity are crucial to facilitate and promote the usability and then the actual practices.

Contributions

This paper provides the following contributions:

- It summarizes the most relevant results provided by telemonitoring solutions, with particular emphasis on multi-agent systems (MAS).
- It details the requirements expressed by the physiotherapists about rehabilitation practices, which to date require the most technological supports.
- It connects the above-mentioned requirements with the offered and potential peculiarities of the envisioned real-time multi-agent systems.
- It discusses innovative challenges for MAS, such as deploying intelligent agents in wearable sensor nodes while facing compliance to strict timing constraints.

Paper structure

The rest of the paper is organized as follows. Section 2 elaborates the state of the art providing a complete overview of both conventional and agent-based telerehabilitation systems. Section 3 presents practices and still unmet requirements expressed by professional physiotherapists. Section 4 discusses strengths and limitations of current agent-based telerehabilitation systems, introducing and detailing the future challenges to be faced by MAS to enhance performance and applicability in rehabilitation scenarios. Finally, Sect. 5 states our conclusions summarizing the lesson learnt and presenting some future work.

2 State of the Art

Telerehabilitation solutions primarily target the elderly and patients from rural areas unable to reach medical centers [12]. Moreover, even in countries with excellent and capillary healthcare systems, telerehabilitation systems are firmly required. For example, in Switzerland, after a surgical intervention, only a limited number of assisted therapy sessions are provided. Thus, employing telerehabilitation systems during unassisted sessions, the follow-up can be fastened enhancing the healing process.

Telerehabilitation is often described as having three primary components *(i)* training and counselling, *(ii)* assessment and monitoring, and *(iii)* point of delivery. *Occupational therapy, physical therapy, and speech-language therapy* [11] are the most provided. However, due to the lack of adequate studies, the interpretation of particular patient groups is restricted [13].

A recovery period, usually about six to eight weeks, can follow an acute trauma (e.g., fall of a fragile elder) or surgical intervention (e.g., joint replacement). This is the most critical period for patients who are luckily still not chronic. Nevertheless, even for the latter, the scientific community provided tailored solutions to relieve pain and maintain or slowly recover physical and/or mental capabilities. Indeed, telerehabilitation targets not only physically impaired [14], but also cognitive impaired patients [15,16] within an average age of 76 (56–91) [13].

The broad range of available technologies enabled the development of various techniques and approaches.

The main category of applications they have generated are based on:

- *video analysis* - mostly involving stereoscopic cameras and image processing algorithms;
- *wearable technology* - mostly focusing on embedded devices and inertial sensors supported by kinematic algorithms;
- *robotics* - mostly focused on in monitoring and motivation involving humanoids or basic robots;
- *distributed sensing* - mostly involving monitoring and reasoning exploiting environmental sensors;
- *gamification* - mostly involving coaching techniques and persuasive technologies.

Despite the considerable availability of extremely precise and complex solutions, telerehabilitation systems have to face user (patients and physiotherapists) acceptability.

The amount of similar proposed solutions suggests that the requirements set from physiotherapists and patients have not yet been entirely met. Factors such as *setup, costs, maintenance, safety, easy usage, minimal set of options and functionalities, and effectiveness* primarily impact on general acceptance or refusal [13].

Iarlori et al. [17] proposed a computer-vision based system applied to patients affected by Alzheimer's disease. The diagnosis of the illness's stage is performed monitoring elderly in their private environment and analyzing personal daily-care activities. Observing the actions listed in the Direct Assessment of Functional Status (DAFS) index and detecting performance's anomalies helps to define the dementia stage. The authors analyzed teeth brushing and hair grooming exploiting a Microsoft Kinect to collect data about the actions observed, tracking and supervising the user's gestures. Thus, the patient can receive an immediate support when incorrect or incoherent behaviors are detected.

Among all of the above, to obtain clinically relevant information, *wearable technology* gained great relevance, being considered as the possible leader of further improvements in both preventative and rehabilitation approaches, while camera-based applications still generate concerns. A study targeting patients in an elderly-care facility revealed that the 93% of the patients accepted body-worn sensor systems, defining them as non-invasive and not affecting normal daily activities [18].

Bergmann et al. [13] reported a surprisingly high consideration among the patients about the aesthetic of wearable sensors, mainly concerned about not appearing *"stigmatized"*. Regarding the physiotherapists, major concerns arose for a restricted recording time due to limited storage capacity, wearability, and reliable real-time feedback.

According to Smith et al. [19], the current wearable devices successfully employed in telerehabilitation can be classified into 3 categories:

- *Microsensors* - capturing health information by using small, intelligent, and low-energy active devices;
- *Wrist devices* - monitoring health information by using combined sensors, display, and wireless transmission in a single solution, which is very convenient for common physical activities;
- *Smart clothes* - capturing information by using thin and flexible health sensors, which have to be compatible with textiles, or made using textile technologies, such as new fibers with specific (mechanical, electrical and optical) properties.

For example, Cesarini et al. [20] provided a highly customizable solution for supporting therapists and patients from the pre-surgical to the rehabilitation phase. Furthermore they presented a particular implementation of a framework, involving two wearable inertial sensors and a tablet, which can precisely monitor the angular position and velocity of the knee joint. Physicians and therapists can define specific exercises and related requirements (e.g., the number of repetitions, the number of steps and angular extension) characterizing the therapy. The system guides the patient during the exercises execution providing a real-time visual feedback on the tablet and evaluating the obtained performance at the end of the session.

Another study presents a real-time feedback system of aquatic-space actions (e.g., performed by swimmers or rehabilitating patients) in the form of a functional sound, exploiting the so-called *sonification* procedure [21]. In particular, such a system is composed of pressure sensors placed on the palmar and dorsal sides of the swimmer's hands, and a water-proof embedded system placed on the back of the swimmer. The pressure signals produced by the swimmer motion are processed by the embedded system and provided in real-time to both swimmer and trainer/therapist. Furthermore, such a system can also be exploited in the context of rehabilitation activities and has already been presented in a specialized conference on aquatic therapy [22]. Therapists have widely accepted it as a promising tool for training and recovery of motor and coordination functions.

Similar solutions, but involving robotic devices in the automation of rehabilitation procedure have been considered helpful in reducing training and rehabilitative sessions of both upper and lower extremities (well-known limitation of conventional methods) [23]. Indeed, task-oriented repetitive movements have a direct positive effect on improving muscle strength and movement in patients with neurological injuries, and automated robotics solutions can acquire a higher number of exercises' repetition compared with conventional approaches [24]. Eriksson et al. [25] realized an autonomous assistive mobile robot that provided monitoring, encouragement, and reminders to aids rehabilitating stroke patients. Navigating autonomously, it monitors the patient's activity of the extremity supposed to be rehabilitating, reminding the patient to follow the program in the case of miss-behaviors. They shown experiments involving post-stroke patients. The proposed approach achieved positive responses about the increasingly active and animated robot behavior. The control system they have used is behavior-based. Such behaviors were characterized as pre- and post-conditions to provide proper real-time feedback.

Jacobs et al. [26] implemented a serious game to support arm-hand rehabilitation for stroke survivors. The main objective was to make the training effective and enjoyable. Exploiting task-oriented training principles, this game requires to manipulate every-day objects, dynamically adapting its difficulty based on the patient's performance. Both physical and cognitive capabilities were involved, and the authors evaluated of two stroke patients over a week.

From a technical and technological point of view, telerehabilitation systems are complex solutions, which have to face context-rich scenarios and uncertainty, handle distributed sources of information, operate in highly dynamic environments with mutual interdependencies and sophisticated distributed controls.

Although classic approaches have been shown as potentially effective, they lack in crucial features such as compatibility, collaboration, coordination, and communication [6].

Indeed, Miranda et al. [27] refer to common incompatibility problems such as data formats (e.g., storing format of 3D images) and different communication protocols. Such systems are either subject at an inevitable abandon, or require integrative upgrades (often unfeasible or requiring a worthless/unaffordable effort).

Therefore, studies such as Bergenti et al. [28] consider multi-agent systems (MAS) a suitable "technology" to realize such applications. Section 2.1 presents the most relevant agent-based telerehabilitation systems.

2.1   MAS for Telerehabilitation

MAS are composed of several agents which are able to communicate with their neighborhoods for computational and decision-making tasks. The agents can share their information using the network interfaces to concur reaching a shared goal. The goal might be consensus, synchronization, or surveillance [23]. Due to these characteristics, MAS have been adopted in several rehabilitation solutions which tried to cope with physical and cognitive rehabilitation or providing specialized models or tools.

Physical rehabilitation

Roda et al. [29] treated elderly motor impairment employing specific devices to control patients movements. Exploiting techniques typical of the Ambient Intelligence (AmI), they proposed a context-aware system integrating diverse devices. Thus, the MAS can react accordingly to the context, supporting physiotherapists in developing new, or adapting already existing therapies precisely tailored to the actual patient needs. Using a Microsoft Kinect, all the motor tasks performed by a patient during the rehabilitation are under control. Moreover, employing third-party sensors they were able to gather oxygen level, posture, gesture, stress, BPM, and mood. Combining such values indexes such as pain or fatigue could also be detected. Physiotherapists expressed fuzzy rules, for example providing a natural way to express how transitions should be made by using linguistic values rather than numerical values. A specific agent equipped with an inference engine elaborates such data while respecting isolation and privacy requirements.

Performing cardiac rehabilitation during its second (sub-acute) and third (intensive outpatient therapy) phase, a large amount of cardiac data (complex and arguably) has to be analyzed in a short period of time. The system proposed by Mesa et al. [30] provides support in data analysis, event classification, and visualization. Such a MAS has been involved in rehabilitative tests such as (i) walking on a treadmill at different speeds and with different slopes; (ii) cycling on a stationary bike at different speeds; (iii) upper body workout; and (iv) lower body workout.

Data and context awareness is considered paramount to establish actual collaboration while interacting with remote participants. Dealing with rehabilitation systems magnifies this challenge. Hence, for both cognitive and physical rehabilitating users, the information awareness is a crucial element to provide patients with a rehabilitation path as tailored as possible [31].

In the context of *Upper Limb Rehabilitation* (ULR), Rodriguez et al. [6] proposed an agent-based system to customize exercises to assist different patients providing a bespoke ULR. A notable peculiarity of such a system is the *context-awareness*, which enables run-time adaptability. Hence, the system "performs" three abstract concurrent tasks: (i) while the patient is executing the exercise for the upper limb, the movements are recorded and monitored; (ii) analyzing specific patient's parameters (e.g., BPM, skin conductance) an agent is in charge of defining the level of stress/fatigue; (iii) the agent behaving as a "virtual therapist" adapts ULR's parameters such as number of repetitions and target area limits according to the current level of stress.

Felisberto et al. [32] developed a MAS that recognizes human movements, identifies human postures, and detects harmful activities in order to prevent risk situations (e.g., sudden diseases and falls). The authors exploited wireless sensor nodes and energy harvesting technologies to realize a wireless body area network (WBAN). On top of that, an intelligent agent constantly analyzes possible profiles variations, aiming at identifying physical and posture deterioration causing accidents.

Robotic manipulators have also been employed in agent-based solutions. Trainees' *learning phases* may be supported by formalizing and enhancing the precision and the input to be understood [23]. Relevant contributions have been provided to the interaction between therapist, trainee, and patient.

In telerehabilitation scenarios, drugs assumption correlated to a highly dynamic environment can be a recurrent situation. Mutingi et al. [10] presented an agent-based decision-making solution for drugs delivering. The bio-physiological signals the authors took into account are blood-pressure, BPM, and respiration. Elaborating the combination of such parameters and drugs therapy may provide to the medical staff important indications about patient and pathology's evolution. Other benefits provided by this solution are staff's workload reduction, increasing resources availability, facilitating the understanding of patients requirements and data collection.

Cognitive Rehabilitation

In the scenario of cognitive rehabilitation, Abreu et al. [16] proposed a set of 3D games to rehabilitate neuropsychiatric disorders. They proposed an automatic agent-based control to facilitate the management of the software processes while the patient is playing.

Known as *"the elderly silent epidemic"*, the Acquired Brain Injury (ABI) requires rehabilitation practices such as visuospatial, memory, functional communication, language, attention, and comprehension training [33]. Roda et al. [34] designed a MAS to *(i)* support the execution of the above-mentioned ABI related therapies, *(ii)* monitor and finally evaluate the performed activities and patient's state (e.g., stress, emotional state, BPM, and oxygen level).

Smith et al. [19] proposed another agent-based solution for functional rehabilitation involving gamification. In an environment away from rehabilitation centers, such a solution promotes a continuous, fun, and stimulating rehabilitation. Such *"games"* have to carefully consider a higher number of variables (e.g., incorporating expertise and motivational capacities of rehabilitation practitioners). Thus, they result in being more complex than the ones offered by off the shelf, which are typically too physically and cognitively challenging for rehabilitation patients. Information about patient compliance and progress are collected and made available to the healthcare specialists for further analysis and considerations. Moreover, the gamification technique has been exploited seeking for an enhancement of the engagement, while performing monitoring and promoting smart learning mechanisms [35].

Other proposed solutions

Providing a platform for interactive learning, Su et al. [36] developed an ontology defining vocabulary, entities and their relationships in rehabilitation medicine. Exploiting an inference engine, existing data can reveal new knowledge having an *"asserted model"* as input and *"inferred model"* as output. Another example of agent-based reasoning is presented in [37]. The authors faced two main challenges: *(i)* scalability - by distributing the reasoning on mobile devices, and *(ii)* penalization by supporting medical staff with a graphical application simplifying the definition of temporal patterns of physiological values.

Liao et al. [38] addressed reliability and security of an agent-based platform for telemonitoring.

Finally, Lai et al. [39] proposed a study involving a community scenario rather than the conventional single patient scenario. The authors evaluated the use of rehabilitation techniques for the post- or chronic-stroke survivors involving video-conferencing solutions. In conclusion, the authors praised efficacy, feasibility, and acceptability of telerehabilitation in community-dwelling stroke clients, recording improvements in both physical and psycho-social wellbeing.

3 Telerehabilitation: Practices and Requirements

Despite the increasing awareness about the effectiveness of telerehabilitation, there is still a lack of high-quality studies evaluating types, components, modality and duration of a therapy, and the long-term functional outcomes [40].

Physiotherapists gain significant experience throughout education, training, and practice. However, the quality of a physiotherapy mainly relies on their experience. The absence of errors, information reproducibility, and simple knowledge sharing [23] still cannot be guaranteed.

According to the study conducted in collaboration with the Institute of Health in Leukerbad, a considerable amount of practices are still carried out with conventional and non-technological methods. Unfortunately, both operators and patients have experienced how easily errors or biases can be introduced in the execution (patient's side) or measurement (physiotherapist's side) of a therapy. Moreover, the use of inadequate tools or systems only complicate the rehabilitation sessions and follow up.

In order to better understand this discrepancy between current practices and physiotherapy with the support of technology, we conducted a study concluding with a questionnaire summarizing several in-person meetings.

The meetings were attended by physicians, therapists, patients and researchers. Their points of view were openly discussed focusing on various rehabilitation practices and current or desired technological supports. The questionnaire consisted of fifteen open questions (listed in the Appendix A) about the most recurring and relevant issues. The topics covered by such questions were organized in five groups:

1. joints requiring rehabilitation, related practices and adjacent limbs involved;
2. rehabilitation environment, and initial causes and conditions;
3. values and parameters that must/might/would be useful to observe;
4. common errors and limits of patients, physiotherapists, current practices and technological solutions;
5. envisioned and desired technological supports.

The outcomes of such a questionnaire are addressed, respecting the structure of the groups above.

First group

The obtained results revealed the body parts that require the most technological support that are the knee, hip, shoulder, neck and back.

Second group

To better understand pre-surgical conditions, rehabilitation environment, and what a system might be required to identify during a prevention phase, the most common causes generating the need for rehabilitation have been investigated. Lifestyle and aging have proven to be the most predominant causes. For example, a sedentary lifestyle might facilitate the development of arthritis/osteoarthritis and early joint degeneration, whilst an intense sportive lifestyle would cause anterior-cruciate ligament or menisci rupture and lower back pain.

Third group

Studying dynamics and physical structures, every body part that might require rehabilitation is connected or contiguous to some other regions. A crucial task is to identify which joints or limbs are eventually involved in the rehabilitation process and require observation. For example, by monitoring the movements of femur and tibia, it is possible to determine the angular interval of the knee during flexion, extension, and abduction. Summarizing the expectation expressed by the physiotherapist community, they require comprehensive solutions supporting the most significant rehabilitation practices and providing measurements if not or enhancing them to better understand:

- therapy and practice adherence;
- performance and correctness of the movements;
- possible adjustments, errors or compensations;
- coaching, encouraging and motivating the patient;
- motivation, commitment, and fatigue measurements;
- specific parameters per practice (e.g., quantification of varus or valgus thrusts during gait or jumps analysis).

Fourth group

Current available solutions in the market present critical lack of usability or information. Devices such as the kinetec [41] help the patient's knee in performing passive and continuous movements. Such a device is usually employed twice per day for a total of two hours during the acute phase[1]. However, the provided information on the knee angle is not precise, because the angle of the machine does not exactly correspond to the angle of the knee. Such a lack of alignment is mostly due to structural reasons, limbs misplacement or attempts to compensate the movement performed by the patient trying to reduce an undetectable pain.

Hence, the system does not offer the possibility of understanding important information such as pain, muscular resistance and patient improvement. Moreover, except for the initial assisted setup, the use of the kinetec is supposed to be unsupervised, thus enabling the propagation of all the aforementioned errors.

---

[1] First phase after a surgical intervention on the knee. It is considered over when the patient is able to passively perform a $90°$ extension.

Fifth group

The *"trust"* in scientific research is a common element emerging in all the participants' answers testifying the firm believing that enhancing traditional practices with technological supports can propel patients towards a faster and better healing process. However, several functionalities are not yet available on the market. Without any form of special commitments, the most required technological interventions are the *(i)* quantifying movements during rehabilitation or sports sessions, *(ii)* accurately measuring joint motor behavior pre-, during, and post-therapeutic intervention, *(iii)* qualitative assessment of the movements complementing quantitative analysis, and finally *(iv)* the measurement of physiological processes (e.g., cells regeneration, muscle growth and activation, blood circulation, and immunosystem condition).

Finally, to better understand the concrete possibilities of technical and technological interventions, it is worth recalling that in the context of rehabilitation, a *therapy* is composed of *activities*, an *activity* consists of *tasks*, and a *task* is a set of *steps* to be performed (e.g., gestural, postural) [34];

Considering their involvement in telerehabilitation systems, interaction tasks can be classified into four categories:

– *Individual task* - a task performed by a single actor (not the system);
– *Collaboration task* - a task carried out by two or more actors, with different or the same roles, in a collaborative way (e.g., the task could not be done without the explicit participation of each actor). Among these actors, we may find the system and/or agents, both humans and non-humans;
– *Communication task* - a task performed by two or more actors, with different or same roles, to exchange information. As in the previous case, among these actors, we may find the system and/or agents, both humans and non-humans;
– *Coordination task* - a task performed by two or more actors, with different or the same roles, that proceed in a coordinated way. As previously, among these actors, we may find the system and/or agents, both respectively human and non-human [6].

To meet the physiotherapists' requirements and thus foster the adoption of MAS in telerehabilitation solutions, Sect. 4 discusses current MAS limitations and future challenges.

4   MAS for Telerehabilitation: Discussion

Although incorporating new technologies into rehabilitation and clinical services delivering achieved a high users' satisfaction [42], this was consistently higher for patients rather than for therapists [9].

Promised advantages brought alongside them several drawbacks. For example, deliberation time seemed to be longer, observation of physiological parameters in several solutions was neglected and was still delegated to the operator.

Fatigue, pain and overall physical state are still not easy to detect and analyze, either by a physiotherapist or a simple embedded system. Thus, a critical analysis can be described as "embedded systems can read and perceive in-loco both vital and kinematic parameters mainly related with *step* and *task* execution (see Sect. 3), but in the case where further analysis is required, heterogeneous and proprietary (so closed) solutions have to be involved. Viceversa, expert agent-based systems can easily provide sophisticated analysis supporting *therapies* and *activities* (see Sect. 3), but cannot be deployed yet on embedded devices".

4.1   Strength

Different patients may represent completely different scenarios. Expert agent-based systems are particularly good at modeling real-world and social systems, where problems are solved in a concurrent and cooperative way without the need of reaching optimal solutions [29]. Therefore, MAS are potentially able to dynamically relate and contextualize vital parameters and rehabilitative practices.

The adoption of MAS is crucial for activities such as *decision making*. Remote diagnosis, treatments adaption and planning, identification of potentially dangerous situations, and knowledge representation and manipulation are the key features common to most rehabilitative scenarios and pervasive cares [29]. Hence, such transparent and intelligent mechanisms might embed in a single comprehensive solution a broad variety of services, only limited by the "number" and "expertise/capabilities" of the involved agents.

Combining all those features, emergency mechanisms could even make decisions in the absence of a human decision maker [10]. The response time (e.g., in terms of data analysis) would be significantly reduced, especially if considering possible accuracy and consistency. However, time guarantees are still a weakness of current MAS.

The next section presents some limitations and their consequences.

4.2   Limitations

The multi-agent paradigm has been embraced to solve several types of problems. However, current MAS cannot yet be predictable and respect strict timing constraints. Hence, it introduces drawbacks related to both the single application and the agent technology itself. For example, in the case of solutions involving robotic operators [23], one of the major problems is represented by a possible need to increase units.

Regarding the multi-agency, the common disadvantages already claimed in the scientific literature [10] are:

- complexity - the higher level of the systems' complexity requires more expertise and training;
- human-relationship - dealing with *"virtual entities"*, patients are concerned about the risk of being disconnected/abandoned by the therapist;

– security - named as *"possible technology perversion"*, this issue refer to ethical and security concerns.

Moreover, analyzing the contributions collected in Sect. 2.1 it is possible to notice the major problems of MAS which inhibit their adoption and limit their benefits.

Figure 1 schematically illustrates the general composition of agent-based rehabilitation systems. Indeed, MAS only appear in the *"higher levels"* of every system. For example, in [30,32] the only sections exploiting agents are the data handler, visualizer, and alert manager. In other contributions, such as [29], references or details about how the agents get information from wearable sensors or embedded devices are missing or omitted.

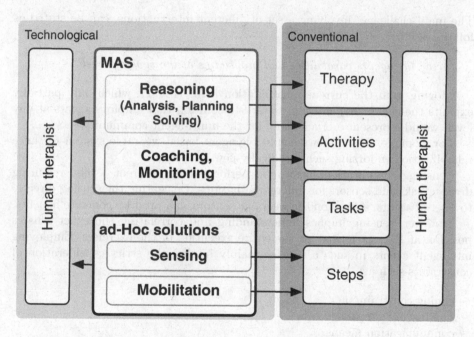

Fig. 1. Rehabilitation MAS structure.

Finally, a study involving a mobile robot hosting a multi-agent platform presented difficulties and barriers related to the use of MAS in embedded devices [43]. The authors presented a mobile robot composed of a Pandaboard, a Discovery STM32, two DC motors and a camera. The MAS running on the Pandaboard was realized using JADE [44] and was in charge of performing all the dynamics related to vision and intelligent planning. However, the robot's motion was managed by the Discovery board (unable to run the MAS and JVM due to limited resources). The "best" solution identified by the authors was to wrap the motion functionality within one of the agents, implementing a custom protocol of communication. The limitations identified by the authors refer to:

- the need for custom communication protocols unable to respect the FIPA standard [45];
- the impossibility of running java-based agent on embedded devices;
- the difficulty of guaranteeing the respect of strict timing constraints;
- the current impossibility of running agent-based systems on real-time operating systems (e.g., Erika Enterprise [46]).

Some radical changes are required to address the limitations listed above. The next section presents the critical challenges specifically required for the telerehabilitation domain.

4.3 Future Challenges

The main challenge, involving a set of different interventions, can be stated as follows:

"bring the agents capabilities and proprieties at the sensing level."

Moving from the current rehabilitation MAS (Fig. 1), which only partially exploits the agents' capabilities, towards a solution that employs agents at any level, would represent a crucial step for the multi-agent community.

For example, Fig. 2 shows a possible agent-based wearable system for knee rehabilitation endorsing such a radically new challenge.

Sensing rehabilitation has to be performed at different levels, requiring diverse tasks and sensors for different situations. Delegating the sensing directly to a set of agents, spread on the wearable sensors, can produce concrete benefits.

However, sensing implies understanding and correlating the exact sensors position at the exact time for the entire execution of the exercises. Employing intelligent agents in such a process mainly implies the strict consideration of constraints such as:

- timing constraints;
- scarcity of resources;
- communication means.

Timing constraints

Current MAS do not yet have mechanisms to deal with *"strict timing constraints"* [47]. In fact, in current implementations, their inner functionalities and interactions do not provide the possibility of facing safety-critical scenarios. As a consequence, a critical failure could lead to injuries, environmental damage, or financial losses. In the case of telerehabilitation, a delayed feedback might increase the risk of a serious injury (e.g., the patient could be requested to continue a movement over the limit of its safety range).

To prevent such risks, the agents involved in such systems have to guarantee the respect of strict timing constraints. Such guarantees are achievable only if, at

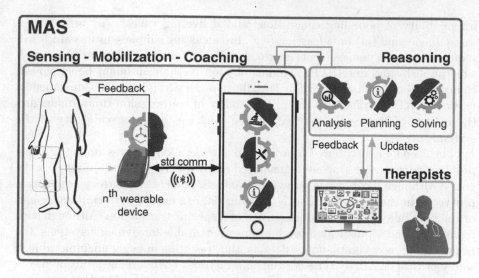

Fig. 2. Agent-based sensing: future challenge for telerehabilitation MAS.

the same time, all the MAS pillars (*the scheduler, the negotiation* and *communication protocols*) consider in their inner mechanisms specific factors [47]. Hence, just having one element of the above incapable of dealing with timing guarantees makes it impossible to provide any guarantee on a predictable behavior.

Agent tasks, usually referred as *behaviours*, can be simple or complex. According to the state of the art, in the most used multi-agent frameworks, they are scheduled with a trivial first-come-first-served (FCFS) approach, while JADE uses a non-preemptive Round-Robin scheduler (NPRR) [48]. Depending on the various behaviour characteristics (e.g., periodic or sporadic), several schedulers typical of real-time embedded systems can be employed. For example, considering to employ schedulers such as Rate Monotonic (RM) [34] or Earliest Deadline First (EDF) [49], based on the analysis of the worst-case scenario for the task-set under evaluation, a correct resource/task allocation and the respect of timing constraints can be guaranteed. In the case of less predictable aperiodic behaviors (e.g., tasks that might generate over-run), the most suitable approach would employ a scheduler based on the concept of *servers* such as the Sporadic Server (SS), Total Bandwidth Server (TBS), and Constant Bandwidth Server (CBS) [49]. Thus, the maximum computation bandwidth of incoming requests can be bounded for each task or class of tasks, providing isolation among them and reducing the pessimism in the timing analysis.

The agent interactions rely on the communication middleware, defining common (possibly standard) formats and semantics. FIPA [45] is the reference standard and it is characterized by messages strictly adhering to the Agent Communication Language (ACL) standard, enabling several possible encoding of the actual contents. Once the message is composed, it is easily sent over IP. However, no mechanism to manage (i) network load and messages status (e.g., the impossibility of bounding congestions and delivering times), (ii) in/out messages queue, and (iii) broadcasting (e.g., broadcasting simple sensors values still require a complex management) is provided. To overcome such limitations, a real-time publish-subscribe (RTPS) communication mechanism might be employed. Hence, systems such as the Data Distribution Service (DDS) [50] implement a version of RTPS to improve the predictability of transmission times, managing the quality of service for the transmitted packages and the scalability of the system.

The need for a distributed coordination of tasks and resources among multiple problem solvers (nodes/agents), generated many different contributions over the years. Although flexibility is always guaranteed, none of the current negotiation protocols, in charge of ruling such distribution, can ensure any temporal bound or the possibility of a positive conclusion of a specific transaction. Although such fascinating and sophisticated mechanisms are suitable for dynamic systems, the negotiation process is still unpredictable, thus resulting in being unemployable in safety-critical or strictly time-dependent scenarios. Therefore, negotiation mechanisms should envision a strict connection with the other MAS components (agent's internal scheduler and communication middleware). For example, the acceptance of a task execution demanded in the negotiation phase impacts on the contractor's task-set (agent proposing for the task execution). In such a way, task-related parameters (e.g., worst-case execution time, inter-arrival time, and activation time) and agent-related parameters (e.g., communication delay and utilization factor) must be mandatorily taken into consideration if aiming at negotiating under real-time constraints. Thus, both tasks already accepted and running on the agent (contractor) and tasks under bids will have ensured the promised response time undertaken during the negotiations.

Scarcity of resources

Most wearable devices have limited resources, such as memory and computational capability, to have a contained impact on the battery lifetime.

Moreover, they are also subject to dimensional restrictions due to wearability and intrusivity factors. Thus, most of the conventional multi-agent frameworks cannot be deployed on such devices. Intervention to lighten agents and communication protocols are envisioned, to finally remove the barriers from the employment of MAS in embedded devices.

Communication means

Wearable devices for telerehabilitation are usually characterized by low-energy consumption communication means, as Bluetooth low-energy (BLE) [51] and Zigbee [52]. Standard communication protocols (e.g., FIPA ACL [45]) need to be updated to suite such new channels of communication. Indeed, broadly used in Ethernet or WiFi connection, such protocols need to take into consideration a new (and more constrictive) set of constraints. Finally, to ensure the respect of *strict timing constraints*, the new communication protocols must take into account boundaries and theories typical of distributed real-time applications.

Facing these new challenges require a substantial intervention within the inner mechanisms of traditional MAS. Nevertheless, the operating principles and basic protocols will still be respected, thus enabling interactions and collaborations with agents implemented according to the current policies. For example, MAS performing *long-term reasoning* and *data handling* operate in non-safety critical scenarios, which still might be implemented in the traditional way. Although incapable of guaranteeing the compliance with the newly presented constraints, such traditional agents can elaborate data provided by the real-time agents running on the wearable devices.

5 Conclusions

This paper presented a comprehensive review and analysis of solutions empowering telerehabilitation. Particular emphasis has been given to agent-based systems, presenting their features, limitations, and new challenges.

Physiotherapist needs and requirements for telerehabilitation have been presented and formalized. Furthermore, the needs still left unsatisfied, with respect to conventional non-technological practices, and inadequate systems on the market, have been highlighted.

Finally, elaborating on existing rehabilitation MAS, the identified strengths are the possibility of *(i)* easy scenarios contextualization, *(ii)* facing uncertainties related to planning and problem solving, *(iii)* coordinating distributed sources of information, and sophisticated distributed controls. Beside these com-proved positive features, limitations such as *(i)* incompatibility with real-time operating systems, *(ii)* impossibility of running agents in embedded devices, and *(iii)* neglect of timing concepts within the agents' ecosystem, claimed the need for new contributions.

The most important new challenges identified in the MAS's future steps are:

(i) implementing time-aware mechanisms into agents' internal scheduler, communication and negotiation protocols,
(ii) coping with scarcity of resources, and
(iii) implementing standard protocols for new communication means.

6 Future Work

According to Amatya et al. [40], rigorous studies are still needed for future research in appropriate outcome measures, optimal intensity, frequency, and cost effectiveness of telerehabilitation intervention over a longer period. Thus, by tightly collaborating with professional physiotherapists and researchers, we aim at facing the identified new challenges bringing the multi-agent features at the sensing level. The first expected outcomes will be primarily a fully distributed and real-time compliant MAS for knee rehabilitation, to then be employed in clinical trials and deliver appropriate studies over an extended period of time.

Acknowledgements. The authors wish to thank the contribution of the COST Action IC1303 - Architectures, Algorithms and Platforms for Enhanced Living Environments (AAPELE).

A   Questionnaire

(1) Which human joints and limbs are your (physiotherapists') primary interest?
(2) What are the most typical causes/conditions? *(e.g., pre-post-surgical, post-stroke, or just aging-related)*

Concerning the joint-limbs, you mentioned in the first question:

(3) How are they treated along the four phases (acute, subacute, chronic, and maintenance)?
(4) Which body parts are involved in the rehabilitation practices?
(5) Which body parts must be (or should be) monitored?

Concerning the previous answers:

(6) Generally, and in your department, which are the most performed/required rehabilitative practices? *(e.g., per body part - type & n. Of test)*
(7) Are they more frequently performed in ambulatory/hospital or a home/home-like environment?
(8) In such practices, what is possible to observe? *(e.g., extension, flexion, n. of repetitions, punctual accuracy)*
(9) In such practices, what is not possible to observe? *(e.g., pain, fatigue, accurate evolution trend)*
(10) In such practices, what should and what shouldn't the patient do? *(e.g., regarding position, execution-speed)*
(11) What are the most common errors typically performed by the patients? *(e.g., compensation)*
(12) What are the most common errors typically performed by the physiotherapists? *(e.g., misreadings)*
(13) What are the (human) patient limits (what should they perceive or understand, but cannot)?
(14) What are the (human) physiotherapist limits (what would you like, but you cannot perceive or understand)?
(15) Concerning the technological research, what do you feel is missing and needs to be implemented?

References

1. Calvaresi, D., Cesarini, D., Sernani, P., Marinoni, M., Dragoni, A.F., Sturm, A.: Exploring the ambient assisted living domain: a systematic review. J. Ambient Intell. Humanized Comput. **8**(2), 239–257 (2017). https://doi.org/10.1007/s12652-016-0374-3
2. Cesarini, D., Calvaresi, D., Marinoni, M., Buonocunto, P., Buttazzo, G.: Simplifying tele-rehabilitation devices for their practical use in non-clinical environments. In: Ortuño, F., Rojas, I. (eds.) IWBBIO 2015. LNCS, vol. 9044, pp. 479–490. Springer, Cham (2015). https://doi.org/10.1007/978-3-319-16480-9_47
3. Hailey, D., Roine, R., Ohinmaa, A., Dennett, L.: Evidence of benefit from telerehabilitation in routine care: a systematic review. J. Telemedicine Telecare **17**(6), 281–287 (2011)
4. Fasola, J., Mataric, M.: A socially assistive robot exercise coach for the elderly. Journal of Human-Robot Interaction **2**(2), 3–32 (2013)
5. Obdržálek, Š., Kurillo, G., Ofli, F., Bajcsy, R., Seto, E., Jimison, H., Pavel, M.: Accuracy and robustness of kinect pose estimation in the context of coaching of elderly population. In: 2012 Annual International Conference of the IEEE Engineering in Medicine and Biology Society, pp. 1188–1193. IEEE (2012)
6. Rodriguez, A.C., Roda, C., González, P., Navarro, E.: Contextualizing tasks in tele-rehabilitation systems for older people. In: Cleland, I., Guerrero, L., Bravo, J. (eds.) IWAAL 2015. LNCS, vol. 9455, pp. 29–41. Springer, Cham (2015). https://doi.org/10.1007/978-3-319-26410-3_4
7. Calvaresi, D., Cesarini, D., Marinoni, M., Buonocunto, P., Bandinelli, S., Buttazzo, G.: Non-intrusive patient monitoring for supporting general practitioners in following diseases evolution. In: Ortuño, F., Rojas, I. (eds.) IWBBIO 2015. LNCS, vol. 9044, pp. 491–501. Springer, Cham (2015). https://doi.org/10.1007/978-3-319-16480-9_48
8. Mozaffarian, D., Benjamin, E.J., Go, A.S., Arnett, D.K., Blaha, M.J., Cushman, M., Das, S.R., de Ferranti, S., Després, J.-P., Fullerton, H.J., et al.: Executive summary: Heart disease and stroke statistics-2016 update: a report from the american heart association. Circulation **133**(4), 447 (2016)
9. Kairy, D., Lehoux, P., Vincent, C., Visintin, M.: A systematic review of clinical outcomes, clinical process, healthcare utilization and costs associated with telerehabilitation. Disabil. Rehabil. **31**(6), 427–447 (2009)
10. Mutingi, M., Mbohwa, C.: Developing multi-agent systems for mhealth drug delivery. In: Adibi, S. (ed.) Mobile Health. SSB, vol. 5, pp. 671–683. Springer, Cham (2015). https://doi.org/10.1007/978-3-319-12817-7_29
11. Morreale, P.A.: Wireless sensor network applications in urban telehealth. In: 21st International Conference on Advanced Information Networking and Applications Workshops, 2007, AINAW 2007, vol. 2, pp. 810–814. IEEE (2007)
12. Li, K.F.: Smart home technology for telemedicine and emergency management. J. Ambient Intell. Humaniz. Comput. **4**(5), 535–546 (2013)
13. Bergmann, J.H.M., McGregor, A.H.: Body-worn sensor design: what do patients and clinicians want? Ann. Biomed. Eng. **39**(9), 2299–2312 (2011)
14. Akdoğan, E., Taçgın, E., Arif Adli, M.: Knee rehabilitation using an intelligent robotic system. J. Intell. Manuf. **20**(2), 195–202 (2009)
15. Chen, J., Zhang, X., Li, R.: A novel design approach for lower limb rehabilitation training robot. In: 2013 IEEE International Conference on Automation Science and Engineering (CASE), pp. 554–557. IEEE (2013)

16. de Abreu, P.F., Werneck, V.M.B., da Costa, R.M.E.M., de Carvalho, L.A.V.: Employing multi-agents in 3-d game for cognitive stimulation. In: XIII Symposium on Virtual Reality, pp. 73–78. IEEE (2011)
17. Iarlori, S., Ferracuti, F., Giantomassi, A., Longhi, S.: Rgbd camera monitoring system for Alzheimer's disease assessment using recurrent neural networks with parametric bias action recognition. IFAC Proc. Volumes **47**(3), 3863–3868 (2014)
18. Fraile, J.A., Bajo, J., Corchado, J.M., Abraham, A.: Applying wearable solutions in dependent environments. IEEE Trans. Inform. Technol. Biomed. **14**(6), 1459–1467 (2010)
19. Smith, S.T., Talaei-Khoei, A., Ray, M., Ray, P.: Agent-based monitoring of functional rehabilitation using video games. In: Brahnam, S., Jain, L.C. (eds.) Advanced Computational Intelligence Paradigms in Healthcare 5, vol. 326, pp. 113–141. Springer, Heidelberg (2010). https://doi.org/10.1007/978-3-642-16095-0_7
20. Cesarini, D., Buonocunto, P., Marinoni, P., Buttazzo, G.: A telerehabilitation framework for lower-limb functional recovery. In: International Conference on Body Area Networks, BodyNets 2014, London, UK. IEEE Computer Society (2014)
21. Cesarini, D., Calvaresi, D., Farnesi, C., Taddei, D., Frediani, S., Ungerechts, B.E., Hermann, T.: Mediation: an embedded system for auditory feedback of hand-water interaction while swimming. Procedia Eng. **147**, 324–329 (2016)
22. Ungerechts, B., Cesarini, D., Wiebel, V., Hermann, T.: Ears drive hands: sonification of liquid effects induced by aquatic space activities contributes to cognitive representation (2015)
23. Adibi, S.: Mobile Health: A Technology Road Map, vol. 5. Springer, Berlin (2015). https://doi.org/10.1007/978-3-319-12817-7
24. Vourvopoulos, A., Liarokapis, F.: Evaluation of commercial brain-computer interfaces in real and virtual world environment: a pilot study. Comput. Electr. Eng. **40**(2), 714–729 (2014)
25. Eriksson, J., Mataric, M.J., Winstein, C.: Hands-off assistive robotics for post-stroke arm rehabilitation. In: Proceedings of the IEEE International Conference on Rehabilitation Robotics (ICORR 2005), pp. 21–24 (2005)
26. Jacobs, A., Timmermans, A., Michielsen, M., Plaetse, M.V., Markopoulos, P.: Contrast: gamification of arm-hand training for stroke survivors. In: CHI 2013 Extended Abstracts on Human Factors in Computing Systems, pp. 415–420. ACM (2013)
27. Miranda, P., Aguilar, J.: A prototype of a multiagents system for a telemedicine environment. Eng. Intell. Syst. Electr. Eng. Commun. **11**(1), 3–8 (2003)
28. Bergenti, F., Poggi, A.: Multi-agent systems for the application and employing of e-health services. In: Cruz-Cunha, M.M., Tavares, A.J., Simoes, R. (eds.) Handbook of Research on Developments in E-Health and Telemedicine: Technological and Social Perspectives, pp. 247–264. IGI Global (2010)
29. Roda, C., Rodríguez, A., López-Jaquero, V., González, P., Navarro, E.: A multi-agent system in ambient intelligence for the physical rehabilitation of older people. In: Bajo, J., Hernández, J.Z., Mathieu, P., Campbell, A., Fernández-Caballero, A., Moreno, M.N., Julián, V., Alonso-Betanzos, A., Jiménez-López, M.D., Botti, V. (eds.) Trends in Practical Applications of Agents, Multi-Agent Systems and Sustainability. AISC, vol. 372, pp. 113–123. Springer, Cham (2015). https://doi.org/10.1007/978-3-319-19629-9_13
30. Mesa, I., Sanchez, E., Diaz, J., Toro, C., Artetxe, A.: Gocardio: a novel approach for mobility in cardiac monitoring. InImpact: J. Innov. Impact **6**(1), 110 (2016)

31. Teruel, M.A., Navarro, E., González, P.: Towards an awareness interpretation for physical and cognitive rehabilitation systems. In: García, C.R., Caballero-Gil, P., Burmester, M., Quesada-Arencibia, A. (eds.) UCAmI 2016. LNCS, vol. 10069, pp. 121–132. Springer, Cham (2016). https://doi.org/10.1007/978-3-319-48746-5_13
32. Felisberto, F., Costa, N., Fdez-Riverola, F., Pereira, A.: Unobstructive body area networks (ban) for efficient movement monitoring. Sensors 12(9), 12473–12488 (2012)
33. Rohling, M.L., Faust, M.E., Beverly, B., Demakis, G.: Effectiveness of cognitive rehabilitation following acquired brain injury: a meta-analytic re-examination of cicerone et al'.s (2000, 2005) systematic reviews. Neuropsychology 23(1), 20 (2009)
34. Roda, C., Rodríguez, A.C., López-Jaquero, V., Navarro, E., González, P.: A multi-agent system for acquired brain injury rehabilitation in ambient intelligence environments. Neurocomputing 231, 11–18 (2017). https://doi.org/10.1016/j.neucom.2016.04.066
35. Li, C., Rusák, Z., Horváth, I., Ji, L.: Validation of the reasoning of an entry-level cyber-physical stroke rehabilitation system equipped with engagement enhancing capabilities. Eng. Appl. Artif. Intell. 56, 185–199 (2016)
36. Su, C.-J., Peng, C.W.: Multi-agent ontology-based web 2.0 platform for medical rehabilitation. Expert Syst. Appl. 39(12), 10311–10323 (2012)
37. Brugués, A., Bromuri, S., Barry, M., Del Toro, Ó.J., Mazurkiewicz, M.R., Kardas, P., Pegueroles, J., Schumacher, M.: Processing diabetes mellitus composite events in magpie. J. Med. Syst. 40(2), 1–15 (2016)
38. Liao, J., Hu, C., Guan, G., Meng, M.Q.-H.: An extensible telemonitoring architecture based on mobile agent method. In: 2009 IEEE International Conference on Robotics and Biomimetics (ROBIO), pp. 1537–1542. IEEE (2009)
39. Lai, J.C.K., Woo, J., Hui, E., Chan, W.M.: Telerehabilitation a new model for community-based stroke rehabilitation. J. Telemedicine Telecare 10(4), 199–205 (2004)
40. Amatya, B., Galea, M.P., Kesselring, J., Khan, F.: Effectiveness of telerehabilitation interventions in persons with multiple sclerosis: a systematic review. Multiple Sclerosis Relat. Disord. 4(4), 358–369 (2015)
41. Beny, L., Griesmar, R.: Device for producing continuous passive motion. US Patent 6,325,770, 4 December 2001
42. Schein, R.M., Schmeler, M.R., Saptono, A., Brienza, D.: Patient satisfaction with telerehabilitation assessments for wheeled mobility and seating. Assistive Technol. 22(4), 215–222 (2010)
43. Calvaresi, D., Sernani, P., Marinoni, M., Claudi, A., Balsini, A., Dragoni, A.F., Buttazzo, G.: A framework based on real-time OS and multi-agents for intelligent autonomous robot competitions. In: 2016 11th IEEE Symposium on Industrial Embedded Systems (SIES), pp. 1–10, May 2016
44. Bellifemine, F.L., Caire, G., Greenwood, D.: Developing multi-agent systems with JADE, vol. 7. Wiley, Chichester (2007)
45. ACL Fipa. Fipa acl message structure specification. Foundation for Intelligent Physical Agents (2002). http://www.fipa.org/specs/fipa00061/SC00061G.html. 30 June 2004
46. Evidence. Erika enterprise rtos. http://www.evidence.eu.com. Accessed September 2017
47. Calvaresi, D., Marinoni, M., Sturm, A., Schumacher, M., Buttazzo, G.: The challenge of real-time multi-agent systems for enabling IoT and CPS. In: Proceedings of IEEE/WIC/ACM International Conference on Web Intelligence (WI 2017), August 2017

48. JADE - Programmer Manual. http://jade.tilab.com/doc/programmersguide.pdf. Accessed 15 May 2017
49. Buttazzo, G.: Hard real-time computing systems: predictable scheduling algorithms and applications, vol. 24. Springer Science & Business Media, Berlin (2011). https://doi.org/10.1007/978-1-4614-0676-1
50. Pardo-Castellote, G.: Omg data-distribution service: architectural overview. In: Distributed Computing Systems Workshops, pp. 200–206. IEEE (2003)
51. Gomez, C., Oller, J., Paradells, J.: Overview and evaluation of bluetooth low energy: an emerging low-power wireless technology. Sensors **12**(9), 11734–11753 (2012)
52. Alliance, Z., et al.: Zigbee specification (2006)

Engineering IoT Systems Through Agent Abstractions: Smart Healthcare as a Case Study

Eloisa Vargiu[1](✉) [iD] and Franco Zambonelli[2] [iD]

[1] eHealth Unit, Eurecat Technology Center, Barcelona, Spain
eloisa.vargiu@eurecat.org
[2] DISMI, Università di Modena e Reggio Emilia, Reggio Emilia, Italy
franco.zambonelli@unimore.it

Abstract. The increasing percentage of elderly people in the population (at least in Europe and North America) is part of a demographic change that will have an enormous impact on the society in the next few years. Thus, intelligent solutions that rely on the Internet of Things have been proposed in the literature, with the final goal to give remote support to elderly people at their home. Those solutions aim at monitoring activities and behaviors, and automatically send alarms in case of anomalies, putting in contact the end-user with her/his GP or alerting the emergency center or familiars, according to the specific needs. However, although the great deal of worldwide researches in the area of the Internet of Things and its early applications to healthcare and tele-assistance, the technologies to apply it in real-world with the necessary dependability levels are far from being assessed. In this paper, we propose novel software engineering concepts that, by synthesizing existing proposals bringing in the lessons of agent-based computing and agent-oriented software engineering, can effectively support the systematic (and thus more dependable) development of Internet of Things applications.

1 Introduction

By 2025, about one-third of Europe's population will be aged 60 years and over, with a particularly rapid increase in the number of people aged 80 years and older. This demographic change will have an enormous impact on the society. Thus, at European and International level, there are powerful arguments for investing in health and well-being as an objective in its own right, but also because the intrinsic relationship to economic growth and competitiveness.

Elderly people aim to preserve their independence and autonomy at their own home as long as possible. However, as they get old the risks of disease and injuries increase making critical to assist and provide them the right care whenever needed. Unfortunately, neither relatives, private institutions nor public care services are viable long-term solutions due to the large amount of required time and cost. In that scenario, several technological solutions have been proposed and adopted: self-management systems for user's empowerment [22]; training systems for elderly people and their family for a better and participatory life [31];

S. Montagna et al. (Eds.): A2HC 2017/A-HEALTH 2017, LNAI 10685, pp. 25–39, 2017.
https://doi.org/10.1007/978-3-319-70887-4_2

social networks to avoid solitude [32]; and teleassistance, to provide remote assistance and support [8]. Focusing on the latter category, a great work has been done to move from pure reactive, unlinked, and not-integrated solutions, to proactive, linked, and integrated-in-the-hospitals solutions.

Early teleassistance efforts were structured mostly as pilot projects that were small in sample size and proof-of-concept in nature, yet they demonstrated that some treatment techniques and rehabilitation assessment could be delivered to end-users located in physically separate locations, thus overcoming obstacles of distance and lack of access to trained providers. In some of the first teleassistance projects, clinicians used the telephone to provide patient's follow-up and caregiver's support, and to administer end-user's self-assessment measures [20,30]. By the late 1980's, this approach expanded to include the use of closed-circuit television and pre-recorded video material to provide visual interaction with end-users [33,34]. Solutions belonging to this first generation of teleassistance systems were totally reactive because assistance was given only in response to a user's request. Moreover, the majority of them only linked to emergency numbers and not directly to GPs of users. Furthermore, they do not allow updating and synchronizing the electronic medical records of the involved end-user, thus providing no integration with the hospital system.

With the advent of low-cost technology, the second generation of teleassistance systems introduced sensors, wearables, and devices (as for instance the panic button) at end-user's homes [16]. In so doing, a direct contact between the end-user and her/his GP is established. Nevertheless, those solutions are still reactive and no integration with the hospital is provided.

In the recent years, novel pro-active solutions have been proposed. In particular, being the final goal to automatically keep the electronic medical record updated in an integrated care perspective, intelligent solutions that rely on nets of sensors and devices have been proposed (third generation of teleassistance) [25]. Those solutions are able to automatically send alarms in case of anomalies, putting in contact the end-user with her/his GP or alerting the emergency center or familiars, according to the specific needs [13]. In particular, there are several of efforts to utilize solutions based on the Internet of Things (IoT) for monitoring elderly people, most of which target only certain aspects of elderly requirements from a limited viewpoint [2,3,7,11,14,15].

However, despite the great deal of worldwide research in the area of the IoT [18] and its applications to several fields [5] – such as teleassistance [27], independent living [12] and, more generally, healthcare [24] – the technologies to apply it in the real world are far from being assessed.

In this paper, we analyze some key general characteristics related to the engineering of complex IoT systems and applications, with a specific focus on the real needs identified in the specific field of teleassistance. Accordingly, we propose novel software engineering abstractions, by synthesizing the common features of existing IoT proposals and application scenarios, and by bringing in the lessons of agent-based computing and agent-oriented software engineering [36]. In our opinion, the adoption of such agent-oriented abstractions can be of help to promote the systematic development of effective and dependable IoT systems, which will be of critical importance in future smart health systems. Indeed, the potential effectiveness is analyzed by adopting a teleassistance scenario as a case study.

2   IoT Systems Engineering: Background Concepts

The definition of general software engineering principles requires identifying the general features and issues that characterize most current approaches to IoT systems design and development.

2.1   Basic Components

The basic components of IoT systems, i.e., the "things", may encompass a large number of physical objects, and also include places and persons.

Physical objects and places can be made trackable and controllable by connecting them to low-cost wireless electronic devices. At the lower end of the spectrum, RFID tags or Bluetooth beacons, based on low-cost and short-range communication protocols, can be attached to any kind of objects to enable tracking their positions and status, and possibly to associate some digital information with them. More advanced devices integrating environmental or motion sensors (i.e., accelerometers) can detect the present and the past activities associated with objects or with some place. In addition, one can make objects actuable –enabling the remote control of their configuration/status via proper digitally-controller actuators– and possibly autonomous –delegating them of autonomously direct their activities. In this perspective, autonomous robots and autonomous objects [1] are components that will increasingly populate the IoT universe.

Concerning persons, other than simply users of the technology, they can also be perceived at first-class entities of the overall IoT vision. Simply having a mobile phone or a wearable device, they can be sensed in their activities and positions, and they can be asked to act in the environment or supply sensing.

2.2   Middleware Infrastructures

To make "things" usable and capable of serving purposes, there is a need of software infrastructures (that is, of IoT middleware [26]) capable both of supporting the "gluing" of different things and of providing some means for stakeholders and users to access the IoT system and take advantage of its functionalities.

Concerning the "glue", there are *interoperability* issues, to enable a variety of very heterogeneous things to interact with each other, via a set of common name spaces, uniform communication protocols and data representation schemes; and *semantic* issues, because a common semantics for concepts must be defined to enable cooperation and integration of things. For both these issues, however, a large body of proposals (dating back to the early years of IoT research) exists. Thus, for our purposes, we assume the existence of proper technical solutions.

Rather, key open "gluing" issues of relevance for software engineering include *discovery, group formation, and coordination*. IoT systems functionalities derive from the orchestrated exploitation of a variety of things, possibly involving a variety of users and stakeholders. Thus, it implies discovering and establishing relations among things, between things and humans, and coordinating their activities also accounting for their social relations [4]. Clearly, for the above coordination mechanisms to work, *context-awareness* and *self-adaptation* are required. In fact, the inherent ephemerality, unreliability, and mobility of system components makes it impossible to anticipate which things will be available and for how long during their exploitation. This requires mechanisms for discovery, group formation, and coordination that are capable of dynamically self-adapting to the general context in which they act, or possibly even self-organize in a context-aware way [21, 37].

Concerning the "access" to the functionalities and capabilities of individual things by users, the scene is currently dominated by the so called "Web of Things" (WoT) vision [17]. The idea is to expose services and functionalities of individual things in terms of REST services, enabling the adoption of assessed Web technologies as far as discovery of things and provisioning of coordinated group services are concerned. Concerning middleware infrastructures, a variety of proposal to support the provisioning of WoT services and applications have appeared [6, 26, 35]. Beside their specificities, most of these proposals rely on: some basic infrastructure to support the WoT approach (i.e., to expose things in terms of simple services); some means to support, in according to a specific coordination model, the discovery of things (and of their associated services), and the coordinated activities of groups of things; and some solutions to make services and applications capable of self-adapting and self-organizing in a context-aware and unsupervised way.

2.3   Services and Applications

With the term "IoT System" we generally refer to the overall set of IoT devices and to the associated middleware infrastructure devoted to manage their networking and their context-aware interactions. Logically above an IoT system, specific software can be deployed to orchestrate the activities of the system so as to provide:

- A number of specific *services*. That is, means to enable stakeholders and users to access and exploit individual things and direct/activate their sensing/actuating capabilities, but also coordinated services that access groups of things and coordinate their sensing/actuating capabilities.
- A number of more general-purpose *applications* or *suites*, intended as more comprehensive software systems intended to both regulate the overall functioning of an IoT system (or of some of its parts), so as to ensure specific overall behavior of the system, as well as to provide an harmonized set of services to access the system and (possibly) its configuration.

Clearly, depending on the specific scenario, one can think of IoT systems in which services may exist only within the context of some general application, but also at scenarios in which there are services that can be deployed as stand-alone.

Based on the above overview of IoT issues, we now try to synthesize the central concepts and abstractions around which the development of IoT systems (spanning analysis and design – implementation issues being mostly out of the scope of this paper) should be centered, and discuss how these directly relate to concepts and abstractions developed in the context of agent-based computing [19, 36].

3   Concepts and Abstractions for IoT System Analysis

The key activities in the analysis of software system-to-be concern *(i)* the identification of the key human actors involved in the usage of the system, and the *(ii)* the identification of the requirements and functionalities to be provided by the system. In this section, we discuss the peculiarities that IoT systems introduce into such activities.

3.1   Human Actors

Identifying the human "actors" of a system-to-be implies identifying those persons/organizations who will own, manage, and/or use the system and its functionalities, and from which requirements should be elicited.

In the case of IoT systems, the distinction between IoT services and applications, and the presence of an IoT middleware to support them and to manage individual things, naturally leads to the identification of three main abstract classes of "actors":

- *Global Managers*: These are the owners of an overall IoT system and infrastructure, or delegates empowered to exert control and establish policies over the configuration, structure, and overall functioning of its applications and services.
- *Local Managers*: These are owners/delegates (whether permanently or on a temporary basis) of a limited portion of the IoT system, empowered to enforce local control and policies for that portion of the system.
- *Users*: These are persons or groups that have limited access to the overall configuration of the IoT applications and services, i.e., cannot impose policies on them, but are nevertheless entitled to exploit services.

The three identified classes of actors are of a very general nature. For example, in a scenario of energy management in a smart city, they could correspond to: city managers, house/shop owners, private citizens and tourists, respectively. In the area of urban mobility, they could correspond to: mobility managers, parking owners or car sharing companies, private drivers, respectively.

3.2   Requirements and Functionalities

Once the key actors are identified, the analysis preceding design and implementation cannot –for IoT systems and applications– simply reduce to elicit from them the functionalities (i.e., the specific services) that things or group of things has to provide, but has to be taken into account for a more comprehensive approach. In fact:

- Beside things provided with basic sensing/actuating functionalities, one should consider the presence of smarter things that can be activated to perform autonomously some long-term activities associated with their nature and with their role in the socio/physical environment in which they situate. These can range from simply cleaning robots to more sophisticated autonomous personal assistants [1].
- IoT applications are not simply concerned with providing a suite of coordinated functionalities, but they should also globally regulate the activities of the IoT systems on a continuous basis, according to the policies established by its stakeholders and to their objectives.

As a consequence, besides analyzing the specific functionalities to deliver, one also has to identify the *policies* and *goals* to be associated with services and applications, i.e., the desirable "state of the affairs" to strive for in the context of the socio-cyber-physical system where IoT applications and services operate.

In this perspective, the general classes of functionalities to be identified for the development of IoT applications and services include:

- *Policies* express desirable permanent configurations or states of functioning of an overall IoT system (global policies) or portions of it (local policies), and have the aims of regulating the overall underlying IoT system. Policies are meant to be always active and actively enforced. Although, from the software engineering viewpoint, the focus is mostly on application-level policies, policies can also account for the proper configuration of the underlying hardware and network infrastructures. The definition of global and local policies is generally in charge of the global managers, although local managers can be also entitled to enforce temporary local policies on local portions of the system (provided they do not contrast with the ones imposed by the global managers).
- *Goals* express desirable situations or state of the affairs that, in specific cases, can/should be achieved. The activation of a goal may rely on specific preconditions (i.e., the occurrence of specific events or the recognition of some specific configurations in the IoT system) or may also be specifically activated upòn user action (e.g., the activation of a goal is invokable "as a service"). The typical post-condition (deactivating the pursuing of a goal) is the achievement of the goal itself. As it was the case for policies, the definition of global and local goals is generally in charge of global, and sometimes of local, managers, whereas users can be sometimes entitled to activate simple local goals (or goals associated to individual things) "as a service".

– *Functions* define the sensing/computing/actuating capabilities of individual things or of group of things, or the specific resources that are to be made available to managers and users in the context of specific IoT applications and services. Functions are typically made accessible in the form of services, and can sometime involve the coordinated access to the functions of a multitude of individual things. Functions and the associated services are typically defined by global and possibly local managers, but are exploited also by the everyday users of the IoT systems.

Clearly, the concepts of goals and policies are central in the research area of agent systems and multiagent systems, and will require, to be realized, components with autonomous and social behaviour, capable of working together towards the achievement of goals and the enforcement of policies.

4 Agent Abstractions for IoT Systems Design

Moving from analysis to the design of an actual system and of its components, one should consider that the "things" to be involved in the implementation of the identified functionalities can correspond to a variety of different objects and devices, other than to places and humans, each relying on a pletora of different technologies and capabilities. Accordingly, from both the gluing software infrastructure and the software engineering viewpoints, it is necessary to define higher-level abstractions to practically and conceptually handle the design and development of application and services, and to harmonically exploit all the components of the IoT system.

Most of the proposal for programming models and middleware acknowledge this need, by virtualizing individual things in some sort of software abstraction [17]. The WoT perspective abstracts things and their functionalities in terms of generic resources, to be accessed via RESTful calls, possibly associating external software HTTP "gateways" to individual things if they cannot directly support HTTP interfacing. Other approaches suggest adopting a more standard SOA or object-oriented approach. Surprisingly, only a few proposals consider associating autonomous software agents to individual things [28], despite the fact goals to be pursued in autonomy may be associated to things, a feature that service-oriented approaches can hardly accommodate.

In addition, as already stated, some "things" make no sense as individual entities as far as the provisioning of specific services and applications is concerned, and are to be considered part of a group and be capable of providing their services as a coordinated group. This applies both to the cases in which a multitude of equivalent devices must be collectively exploited abstracting from the presence of the individuals [6], and to the cases in which the functionalities of the group complement with each other and needs to be orchestrated [28]. However, due to the dynamic and contextual nature of IoT scenario, traditional service-oriented orchestration methods, although necessary, are not enough.

With these considerations in mind, in an effort of synthesizing from a variety of different proposals and of bringing in as needed agent-oriented concepts, we suggest the unifying abstractions of *avatars* and *coalitions* (see Fig. 1).

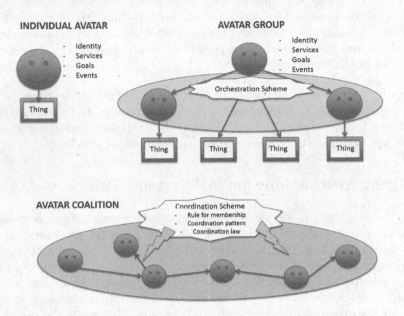

Fig. 1. Avatars, groups, and coalitions.

4.1   Avatars

Borrowing the term from [23] (to distinguish from software agents but nevertheless borrowing several features from them) we define an avatar as the general abstraction for individual things and also for group of things (and possibly other avatars) that contribute to define a unique functionality/service. Avatars abstract away form the specific physical/social/technological characteristics of the things their represent, and are defined by means of:

- *Identity.* An avatar has a unique identity and is addressable. An avatar representing a group does not necessarily hides the identities of inner avatars, but it has its own identity.
- *Services.* These represent access point for exploiting the peculiar capabilities of avatars. That is, depending on the kinds of things and functionalities a service abstracts: triggering and directing the sensing/computing/actuating capabilities, or accessing some managed resources.
- *Goals.* Goals, in the sense of desired state of the affairs, can be associated to avatars. A goal may have a pre-condition for autonomous activation, or may be explicitly activated by a user or by another avatar.

- *Events*. Events represent specific state of the affairs that can be detected by an avatar, and that may be of interests to other avatars or to users. Other avatars or users can subscribe to events of interest.

Clearly, for group of avatars, an internal *orchestration scheme* must be defined for coordinating the activities/functionalities of the things (or of the other avatars) it includes. In general terms –and in accordance with assessed service-oriented approaches– an orchestration scheme defines the internal work-flow of activities among the composing things and avatars, and the con-strains/conditions they are subjected to. Orchestration scheme may also account for contextual information, to make the activities of the group of context-aware. The need of defining orchestrations schemes and constraints to rules the access and usage of (group of) things is generally attributed –with specific character-istics and terminologies– in most middleware and programming approaches for IoT [6,35].

The avatar abstraction is in line, and account for all the typical character-istics, of most existing IoT approaches. However, the stateful concepts of goals and events make avatars go beyond RESTful approaches. Indeed, these con-cepts make an avatar more than simply a service provider, turning it into an autonomous entity capable of goal-oriented and situated behaviour. Although most existing approaches recognize the need to somehow incorporate similar concepts within RESTful architectures [17], a few of them explicitly refer to agent-based computing, where such concepts belong to.

4.2 Coalitions

Without fear of borrowing the term from the area of multiagent systems [10], we define a coalition as a group of avatars that coordinates each other's activities in order to reach specific goals, or enact specific policies. Accordingly, coalitions may be of a temporary or permanent nature. Unlike avatar groups, coalitions do not necessarily have an identity, and do not necessarily provide services.

To define and bring a coalition in action, the abstraction of coalition must be defined (at least) in terms of a *coordination scheme* that should include:

- *Rules for membership*, to specify the conditions upon which an avatar should/could enter a coalitions. From the viewpoint of individual avatars, the act of entering a coalition can be represented by the activation of a specific goal based on pre-conditions that correspond to the rules for membership [9].
- *Coordination pattern*, to define the pattern (interaction protocol and shared strategy) by which the members of the coalition have to interact. The coor-dination pattern may include an explicit representation of the goal by which the coalition has been activated. However, such goal can also be implicit in the definition of the protocol and of the strategy.
- *Coordination law*, to express constraints that must be enforced in the way the avatars involved in the coalition should act and interact.

In addition, one can consider the possibility to subscribe to events occurring within the coalition.

The view of avatar coalitions can be used to realize policies, or to aggregate groups of avatar based on similarity, so as to make them work collectively in a mission-oriented way without forcing them to follow a specific identity-centered orchestration schema. This is coherent with the idea of multiagent societies and, in general, of distributed dynamic coordination [19]. Also, this is in line with nature-inspired approaches [37], and approaches to aggregate programming.

The main software engineering concepts discussed in this Section are graphically frames in a logical stack in Fig. 2.

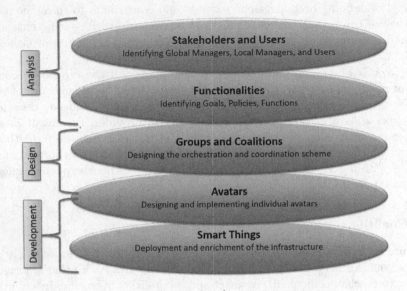

Fig. 2. Key concepts and abstractions for IoT engineering.

5   A Real World Case Scenario: Teleassistance

In third generation teleassistance, IoT enriches houses to support smart health monitoring and care. Thus, houses are densely augmented with connected sensors and actuators: light and heat controllers, gas and smoke detectors, presence and motion sensors, door (main doors, internal doors, fridge, kitchen furniture) sensors, electric consume sensors, shutter/curtain controller, as well as sensorized everyday objects (e.g., cup, fork, cane). Suitable "things" may become smart to accomplish this goal:

- RFID tags may be attached to everyday objects in houses such as glasses to detect the quantity of ingested water;
- suitable controllers (e.g., Arduino-based) may be integrated in order to enable turning on/off the light in a specific room remotely (e.g., via a mobile phone);

- autonomous systems that may open and close the shutter/curtain depending on the performed activities, the context (the hour, the day), and/or user's habits;
- robots may be leveraged for additional assistance (e.g., the Giraff plus [29]).

Moreover, also medical devices (e.g., pulse-oximetry, smart scale) may be provided to elderly people in order to automatically send health status information and measures.

In such a scenario, different actors (from medical doctors to elderly people and their family members) can contribute to set up a variety of IoT services to support both medical doctors in the monitoring and care activities of individuals, and to help individuals and their family members in their everyday self-managed healthcare activities.

Functionalities have to be provided fusing together different things and, possibly, involving different users and stakeholders. For instance, it is desirable to automatically configure a given room (e.g., bedroom) for a given context (e.g., time to go to sleep). This implies a discovery service able to detect the right devices (e.g., the bedroom light actuator) among those belonging to the overall lightening and shutter system. Moreover, coordination is needed to ensure that all the involved devices act in accordance (e.g., if is time to go to sleep, the bedroom light must be turned off if the end-user is on the bed through the coordination with the mattress sensor). Context-awareness is also required to actuate when some pre-conditions are triggered (e.g., the end-user is on the bed and it is 10:00 PM) taking also into account that the context may change according to recommendations by caregivers and clinicians (e.g., caregiver may suggest to not to go to sleep a specific day for medical reasons) guaranteeing self-adaptation.

Concerning the general classes of functionalities listed above, in teleassistance we may identify:

- Global and local policies may be defined. For instance, a policy could be introduced to specify the maximum sleeping hours at day or the maximum allowed time for sedentary activities. Policy compliance may be verified relying on the system, for instance, not-intrusive sensors may monitor activities and invite elderly people to be more active or, on the contrary, to go for resting whenever needed.
- Goals to be automatically achieved to give support and assistance, especially in emergency situation. One example could be that of activating an evacuation procedure upon detection of fire by a smoke sensor (pre-conditions), whose goal (and post-condition) is to achieve a quick evacuation of the patient from her/his home. To this end, the activation of a goal can trigger the activities of digital signages and controllable doors in order to rationally guide people towards the exits. Another example could be the case of a fall has been detected. An audio sensor automatically recognizes the help request by the patient (pre-conditions), whose goal is to immediately send assistance at home (e.g., an ambulance) and to communicate with the familiars to make a visit and support the patient (post-condition). To this end, the activation of a goal can trigger the activities of contacting caregivers and familiars.

– Both individual and complex functions should be required: a door sensor in a fridge, e.g., to control opening/closing (individual); or to control the content of the fridge to update the shopping list accordingly (complex).

Finally, let us consider stakeholders and users in the teleassistance scenario:

– Global managers: system managers devoted to control the overall IoT system of the smart houses set according to the directives of the medical doctors, e.g., for deciding heating levels or for surveillance strategies;
– Local managers: house owners, empowered to control the IoT system in their houses and rooms, and tune the local parameters and exploit its services according to own specific needs;
– Users: elderly people with limited abilities, authorized to access specific services (e.g., regulating specific appliances), but not entitled to modify the overall configuration of their houses (in charge of medical doctors and partly of their responsible family members).

Figure 3 shows the different roles of IoT actors in defining and exploiting the above framed functionalities in the teleassistance scenario.

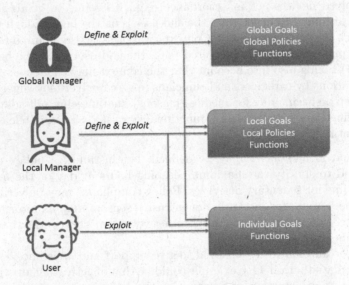

Fig. 3. IoT actors and the functionalities of IoT systems.

6   Conclusions and Future Directions

Third generation teleassistance aims to provide remote support and online help to people that need assistance, as elderly people. Several solutions aimed at monitoring elderly people and their homes have been presented in the literature, most of them based on the IoT technology. In this scenario, this paper proposed and framed some key conceptual abstractions revolving around the IoT universe and showed how they may apply to the teleassistance scenario. The abstractions presented in the paper together with their implementation in this specific scenario represent a first small step towards a general discipline for engineering IoT systems and applications.

As future directions, we are currently defining the overall infrastructure required to put in practice the concepts illustrated and discussed in the paper in order to start testing its real application in teleassistance. Once infrastructure and the basic concepts will be implemented, their effectiveness will be evaluated through a living-lab approach.

Acknowledgments. The study was partially funded by the European Community under "H2020-EU.3.1. - Societal Challenges - Health, demographic change and well-being" programme, project grant agreement number 689802 (CONNECARE).

References

1. Agrawal, H., Leigh, S., Maes, P.: L'evolved: autonomous and ubiquitous utilities as smart agents. In: ACM International Joint Conference on Pervasive and Ubiquitous Computing, pp. 487–491. ACM, New York (2015)
2. Anliker, U., Ward, J.A., Lukowicz, P., Tröster, G., Dolveck, F., Baer, M., Keita, F., Schenker, E.B., Catarsi, F., Coluccini, L., et al.: Amon: a wearable multiparameter medical monitoring and alert system. IEEE Trans. Inf. Technol. Biomed. **8**(4), 415–427 (2004)
3. Atallah, L., Lo, B., Ali, R., King, R., Yang, G.Z.: Real-time activity classification using ambient and wearable sensors. IEEE Trans. Inf. Technol. Biomed. **13**(6), 1031–1039 (2009)
4. Atzori, L., Carboni, D., Iera, A.: Smart things in the social loop: paradigms, technologies, and potentials. Ad Hoc Netw. **18**, 121–132 (2014). http://dx.doi.org/10.1016/j.adhoc.2013.03.012
5. Bandyopadhyay, D., Sen, J.: Internet of things: applications and challenges in technology and standardization. Wirel. Pers. Commun. **58**(1), 49–69 (2011)
6. Beal, J., Pianini, D., Viroli, M.: Aggregate programming for the internet of things. IEEE Comput. **48**(9), 22–30 (2015). http://doi.ieeecomputersociety.org/10.1109/MC.2015.261
7. Bidargaddi, N., Sarela, A., et al.: Activity and heart rate-based measures for outpatient cardiac rehabilitation. Methods Inf. Med. **47**(3), 208–216 (2008)
8. Bower, P., Cartwright, M., Hirani, S.P., Barlow, J., Hendy, J., Knapp, M., Henderson, C., Rogers, A., Sanders, C., Bardsley, M., et al.: A comprehensive evaluation of the impact of telemonitoring in patients with long-term conditions and social care needs: protocol for the whole systems demonstrator cluster randomised trial. BMC Health Serv. Res. **11**(1), 184 (2011)
9. Bures, T., Plasil, F., Kit, M., Tuma, P., Hoch, N.: Software abstractions for component interaction in the internet of things. Computer **49**(12), 50–59 (2016)
10. Cao, Y., Yu, W., Ren, W., Chen, G.: An overview of recent progress in the study of distributed multi-agent coordination. IEEE Trans. Industr. Inform. **9**(1), 427–438 (2013)
11. Chan, M., Campo, E., Estève, D.: Assessment of activity of elderly people using a home monitoring system. Int. J. Rehabil. Res. **28**(1), 69–76 (2005)

12. Dohr, A., Modre-Opsrian, R., Drobics, M., Hayn, D., Schreier, G.: The internet of things for ambient assisted living. In: 2010 Seventh International Conference on Information Technology, pp. 804–809. IEEE (2010)

13. Fernández, J.M., Solà, M., Steblin, A., Vargiu, E., Miralles, F.: The Relevance of providing useful and personalized information to therapists and caregivers in tele*. In: Lai, C., Giuliani, A., Semeraro, G. (eds.) Information Filtering and Retrieval. SCI, vol. 668, pp. 97–117. Springer, Cham (2017). https://doi.org/10.1007/978-3-319-46135-9_6

14. Franco, C., Demongeot, J., Villemazet, C., Vuillerme, N.: Behavioral telemonitoring of the elderly at home: detection of nycthemeral rhythms drifts from location data. In: 2010 IEEE 24th International Conference on Advanced Information Networking and Applications Workshops (WAINA), pp. 759–766. IEEE (2010)

15. Gokalp, H., Clarke, M.: Monitoring activities of daily living of the elderly and the potential for its use in telecare and telehealth: a review. Telemed. eHealth 19(12), 910–923 (2013)

16. Gupta, G.S., Mukhopadhyay, S., Sutherland, M., Demidenko, S.: Wireless sensor network for selective activity monitoring in a home for the elderly. In: Instrumentation and Measurcment Technology Conference Proceedings (IMTC 2007), pp. 1–6. IEEE (2007)

17. Heuer, J., Hund, J., Pfaff, O.: Toward the web of things: applying web technologies to the physical world. Computer 48(5), 34–42 (2015)

18. Iansiti, M., Lakhani, K.: Digital ubiquity: how connections, sensors, and data, are revolutionizing business. Harv. Bus. Rev. 92, 90–99 (2014)

19. Jennings, N.R.: An agent-based approach for building complex software systems. Commun. ACM 44(4), 35–41 (2001). http://doi.acm.org/10.1145/367211.367250

20. Korner-Bitensky, N., Wood-Dauphinee, S.: Barthel index information elicited over the telephone: is it reliable? Am. J. Phys. Med. Rehabil. 74(1), 9–18 (1995)

21. Kott, A., Swami, A., West, B.: The internet of battle things. Computer 49(12), 70–75 (2016)

22. Lorig, K.R., Holman, H.R.: Self-management education: history, definition, outcomes, and mechanisms. Ann. Behav. Med. 26(1), 1–7 (2003)

23. Mrissa, M., Medini, L., Jamont, J.P., Le Sommer, N., Laplace, J.: An avatar architecture for the web of things. IEEE Internet Comput. 19(2), 30–38 (2015)

24. Rafael-Palou, X., Steblin, A., Vargiu, E.: Remotely supporting patients with obstructive sleep apnea at home. In: Ahmed, M.U., Begum, S., Raad, W. (eds.) HealthyIoT 2016. LNICSSITE, vol. 187, pp. 119–124. Springer, Cham (2016). https://doi.org/10.1007/978-3-319-51234-1_19

25. Rafael-Palou, X., Zambrana, C., Dauwalder, S., de la Vega, E., Vargiu, E., Miralles, F.: Third generation teleassistance: intelligent monitoring makes the difference. In: 2nd Workshop on Artificial Intelligence and Internet of Things (AI-IoT) @ECAI 2016, The Hague, 30 August 2016, CEUR Workshop Proceedings, vol. 1724, pp. 1–6 (2016)

26. Razzaque, M.A., Milojevic-Jevric, M., Palade, A., Clarke, S.: Middleware for internet of things: a survey. IEEE Internet Things J. 3(1), 70–95 (2016)

27. Rivero-Espinosa, J., Iglesias-Pérez, A., Gutiérrez-Dueñas, J.A., Rafael-Palou, X.: Saapho: an AAL architecture to provide accessible and usable active aging services for the elderly. ACM SIGACCESS Access. Comput. 107, 17–24 (2013)

28. Spanoudakis, N., Moraitis, P.: Engineering ambient intelligence systems using agent technology. IEEE Intell. Syst. 30(3), 60–67 (2015)

29. Ullberg, J., Loutfi, A., Pecora, F.: A customizable approach for monitoring activities of elderly users in their homes. In: Mazzeo, P.L., Spagnolo, P., Moeslund, T.B. (eds.) AMMDS 2014. LNCS, vol. 8703, pp. 13–25. Springer, Cham (2014). https://doi.org/10.1007/978-3-319-13323-2_2

30. Vaughn, G.: Tel-communicology: health-care delivery system for persons with communicative disorders. Asha **18**(1), 13–17 (1976)

31. Warsi, A., Wang, P.S., LaValley, M.P., Avorn, J., Solomon, D.H.: Self-management education programs in chronic disease: a systematic review and methodological critique of the literature. Arch. Internal Med. **164**(15), 1641–1649 (2004)

32. Wenger, G.C.: Social networks and the prediction of elderly people at risk. Aging Mental Health **1**(4), 311–320 (1997)

33. Wertz, R.T., Dronkers, N.F., Bernstein-Ellis, E., Shubitowski, Y., Elman, R., Shenaut, G.K.: Appraisal and diagnosis of neurogenic communication disorders in remote settings. Clin. Aphasiol. **17**, 117–123 (1987)

34. Wertz, R.T., Dronkers, N.F., Bernstein-ellis, E., Sterling, L.K., Shubitowski, Y., Elman, R., Shenaut, G.K., Knight, R.T., Deal, J.L.: Potential of telephonic and television technology for appraising and diagnosing neurogenic communication disorders in remote settings. Aphasiology **6**(2), 195–202 (1992)

35. Yao, L., Sheng, Q., Dustdar, S.: Web-based management of the internet of things. IEEE Internet Comput. **19**(4), 60–67 (2015)

36. Zambonelli, F., Omicini, A.: Challenges and research directions in agent-oriented software engineering. Auton. Agents Multi Agent Syst. **9**(3), 253–283 (2004)

37. Zambonelli, F., Omicini, A., Anzengruber, B., Castelli, G., Angelis, F.L.D., Serugendo, G.D.M., Dobson, S., Fernandez-Marquez, J.L., Ferscha, A., Mamei, M., Mariani, S., Molesini, A., Montagna, S., Nieminen, J., Pianini, D., Risoldi, M., Rosi, A., Stevenson, G., Viroli, M., Ye, J.: Developing pervasive multi-agent systems with nature-inspired coordination. Perv. Mobile Comput. **17, Part B**, 236–252 (2015)

Event Calculus Agent Minds Applied to Diabetes Monitoring

Nicola Falcionelli[1](✉), Paolo Sernani[1], Albert Brugués[2],
Dagmawi Neway Mekuria[1], Davide Calvaresi[2,3], Michael Schumacher[2],
Aldo Franco Dragoni[1], and Stefano Bromuri[4]

[1] Università Politecnica delle Marche, Ancona, Italy
{n.falcionelli,d.n.mekuria}@pm.univpm.it,
{p.sernani,a.f.dragoni}@univpm.it
[2] University of Applied Sciences Western Switzerland, Sierre, Switzerland
{albert.brugues,michael.schumacher}@hevs.ch
[3] Scuola Superiore Sant'Anna, Pisa, Italy
d.calvaresi@sssup.it
[4] Open University of the Netherlands, Heerlen, The Netherlands
stefano.bromuri@ou.nl

Abstract. The increasing incidence of chronic diseases is a major challenge for the healthcare sector. Personal Health Systems (PHSs) address the self-management of chronic diseases, by decentralizing the health monitoring outside hospitalized environments. Rule based agents allow bringing domain experts' knowledge into PHSs. However, agents must meet the requirements of real monitoring scenarios, characterized by massive streams of events. Hence, with the aim to monitor the health status of diabetic patients, two logic-based agent minds for an agent-oriented PHS are presented. One agent mind is based on the standard version of jREC, a Prolog-based implementation of Cached Event Calculus, while the other is a customization of the standard jREC mind that exploits an event-indexing technique. Both of them are as well integrated into MAGPIE, a Java agent platform. The paper then compares and analyzes the performance of the proposed agent minds, by computing the time needed to trigger different type of alerts, when the number of recorded events (e.g. values of physiological parameters) increases. The results show that the customized jREC mind performs much better when a high number of events need to be checked, making its use advisable in monitoring scenarios.

1 Introduction

The incidence of chronic diseases in the population is recognized as a major challenge for the healthcare sector [2]. For instance, the number of people affected by diabetes has doubled in the last 20 years [33]. Statistics from WHO report that more than 400 million individuals live with diabetes, and losses in the GDP for diabetes-related costs from 2011 to 2030 are estimated at 1.7 trillion USD [32].

© Springer International Publishing AG 2017
S. Montagna et al. (Eds.): A2HC 2017/A-HEALTH 2017, LNAI 10685, pp. 40–56, 2017.
https://doi.org/10.1007/978-3-319-70887-4_3

Personal Health Systems (PHSs) aim at supporting the self-management of chronic diseases and reducing the healthcare costs by supporting medical doctors in following the patients' disease evolution [10]. PHSs implement the *"healthcare to anyone, anytime, and anywhere"* paradigm, by increasing both the coverage and the quality of healthcare [31]. In fact, PHSs bring the health technology to domestic environments, by customizing healthcare services to the specific needs, practices, and situations of people and their social contexts [24]. PHSs ensure the continuity of care, focusing on a knowledge-based approach integrating past and current data of each patient together with statistical evidence [29]. A PHS is composed of three tiers [30]: Tier 1 is the Body Area Network (BAN), i.e. the set of sensors on the patient's body to monitor her health parameters; Tier 2 is the personal server, usually a mobile device, which collects and aggregates the parameters and events produced by the BAN; Tier 3 is the remote server which processes and stores the data from the personal server and supports doctors in following the treatment of patients at home.

In addition to the modeling capabilities of agent-based frameworks [28] and despite their still opened challenges [12,13], Multi-Agent Systems have been proved useful in the healthcare sector implementing modularity, distribution, and personalization for data management, decision support systems, planning and resource allocation, and remote care [18], thus being ideal for PHSs. An agent-based platform called MAGPIE [8] implements a programmable expert PHS to monitor patients suffering from diabetes. In particular, that agent platform adds scalability to the PHS by shifting from Tier-3 to Tier-2 the computation needed for the patient monitoring. To obtain such scalability, the agents, composed by an agent body and an agent mind, run directly on the personal server. The agent body is the part of the agent that collects the data acting as an interface between the BAN in Tier-1 and the agent mind. The agent mind, based on an Event Calculus (EC) engine, is the part of the agent that checks the data collected from the body to perform the monitoring task and trigger alerts for the medical doctors in Tier-3. The approach of MAGPIE allows improving the scalability of the PHS when the number of patients increases, compared to a centralized PHS where the computation is performed in Tier-3. However, another aspect has to be taken into account: the scalability of the agent mind when the number of events increases. In fact, the use of rule engines based on EC usually restricts the number of events and rules to be considered in a real monitoring scenario, where short time delays are needed to apply corrective actions. Thus, the next step to apply the agent-based PHS in real scenarios requiring long-term monitoring is to develop agent minds capable of caching and retrieving events efficiently.

This paper addresses such issue by proposing two agent minds for the MAG-PIE agent platform presented in [8]. The agent minds have been implemented using jREC, a Cached Event Calculus (CEC) reasoner based on Java and tuProlog [5], to move the computational complexity from query to update time by caching the maximum validity intervals for fluents (i.e. a condition or a property that can change over time). Even though both are based on jREC and integrated into the MAGPIE agent platform, the proposed agent minds differ on the way in which they handle event streams. One is a straightforward integration of the jREC engine, and the other is based on an indexing technique that gives to jREC the ability to process event streams more efficiently.

In addition, as the main contribution of the paper, the performance of the jREC-based agent minds are evaluated on the time required to trigger an alert, when the number of events generated by the agent body increases. Diabetes has been adopted as the use case for the monitoring rules to be checked.

The rest of the paper is organized as follows. Section 2 presents the paper background on EC, CEC, jREC and red-black trees (a balanced binary search tree used here for efficient event indexing). Section 3 describes an overview of the entire PHS in which the agent minds runs, shows the encoding of the monitoring rules to check alerts based on glucose and blood pressure levels in diabetic patients, as well as problems and solutions that arise when massive streams of events have to be handled by reasoning engines. Section 4 presents the experimental results to evaluate the two agent minds. Section 5 describes the work related to the presented research. Section 6 draws the conclusions of the paper and outlines the future work.

2   Background

This section introduces the concepts on which the proposed agent minds are based on.

2.1   Event Calculus

EC is a logic formalism for reasoning about actions and their effects in time [20]. Therefore, it is a suitable tool for modeling expert systems representing the evolution in time of an entity by means of the production of events. EC is based on many-sorted first-order predicate calculus, known as domain-independent axioms, which are represented as normal logic programs that are executable in Prolog. The underlying time model of EC is linear. EC manipulates fluents, where a fluent represents a property that can have different values over time. The term $F = V$ denotes that a fluent F has value V as a consequence of an action that took place at some earlier time-point and not terminated by another action in the meantime. Table 1 summarizes the main EC predicates. Predicates, functions, symbols and constants start with lowercase letter, while variables start with uppercase letter. Predicates in the text are referenced as predicate/N, where predicate is the name of the predicate and N its arity (e.g. number of arguments).

The domain independent axioms of EC are the following:

$$\text{holdsAt}(F = V, 0) \leftarrow \text{initially}(F = V). \tag{1}$$

$$\begin{aligned}
\text{holdsAt}(F = V, T) \leftarrow \\
\text{initiatesAt}(F = V, T_s), T_s < T, \\
\text{not broken}(F = V, [T_s, T]).
\end{aligned} \tag{2}$$

Table 1. Main event calculus predicates

Predicate	Meaning
initially(F = V)	The value of fluent F is V at time 0
holdsAt(F = V,T)	The value of fluent F is V at time T
holdsFor(F = V,[T_{min}, T_{max}])	The value of fluent F is V between T_{min} and T_{max}
initiatesAt(F = V,T)	At time T the fluent F is initiated to have value V
terminatesAt(F = V,T)	At time T the fluent F is terminated from having value V
broken(F = V,[T_{min}, T_{max}])	The value of fluent F is either terminated at T_{max}, or initiated to a different value than V between T_{min} and T_{max}
happensAt(E,T)	An event E takes place at time T updating the state of the fluents

Predicate (1) states that a fluent F holds value V at time 0, if it has been initially set to this value. For any other time T > 0, the predicate (2) states that the fluent holds at time T if it has been initiated to value V at some earlier time point T_s, and it has not been broken on the meanwhile.

$$broken(F = V, [T_{min}, T_{max}]) \leftarrow$$
$$terminatesAt(F = V, T), T_{min} < T, T_{max} > T. \tag{3}$$

$$broken(F = V_1, [T_{min}, T_{max}]) \leftarrow$$
$$initiatesAt(F = V_2, T), V_1 \neq V_2, \tag{4}$$
$$T_{min} < T, T_{max} > T.$$

Predicates (3) and (4) specify the conditions that break a fluent. Predicate (3) states that a fluent is broken between two time points Tmin and Tmax if within this interval it has been terminated to have value V. Alternatively, predicate (4) states that a fluent is broken within a time interval if it has been initiated to hold a different value.

$$holdsFor(F = V, [T_{min}, T_{max}]) \leftarrow$$
$$initiatesAt(F = V, T_{min}),$$
$$terminiatesAt(F = V, T_{max}), \tag{5}$$
$$not\ broken(F = V, [T_{min}, T_{max}]).$$

$$holdsFor(F = V, [T_{min}, +\infty]) \leftarrow$$
$$initiatesAt(F = V, T_{min}), \tag{6}$$
$$not\ broken(F = V, [T_{min}, +\infty]).$$

$$\text{holdsFor}(F = V, [-\infty, T_{max}]) \leftarrow$$
$$\text{terminatesAt}(F = V, T_{max}), \qquad (7)$$
$$\text{not broken}(F = V, [-\infty, T_{max}]).$$

Predicates (5), (6) and (7) deal with the validity intervals of fluents. In particular, predicate (5) specifies that a fluent F keeps value V for a time interval going from $Tmin$ to $Tmax$ if nothing happens in the middle that breaks such an interval. Predicates (6) and (7) behave in the same way, but deal with open intervals.

The domain dependent predicates in EC are typically expressed in terms of the initiatesAt/2 and terminatesAt/2 predicates. One example of a common rule for initiatesAt/2 is

$$\text{initatesAt}(F = V, T) \leftarrow$$
$$\text{happensAt}(Ev, T), \qquad (8)$$
$$Conditions[T].$$

The above definition states that a fluent is initiated to value V at time T if an event Ev happens at this time point, and some optional conditions depending on the domain are satisfied. In relation with MAGPIE, the agent platform in which the proposed agent mind has been integrated, these events that must happen are physiological measurements from the patient.

2.2   Cached Event Calculus and jREC

Straightforward implementations of EC [20] have time and memory complexity which are not practical for developing real applications. This is due to the fact that every time the EC engine is queried, the computation starts from scratch, and all fluents validity intervals are calculated again. Cached Event Calculus (CEC), proposed by Chittaro and Montanari [14], tries instead to overcome this inefficiency by giving EC a memory mechanism, and moving computation from query time to update time.

CEC formalizes the concept of Maximal Validity Interval (MVI), that represents a time interval in which a particular fluent holds without being terminated by any event. A fluent is also associated to a list of MVIs, in order to express all the time intervals in which that fluent holds continuously.

Whenever the rule engine is updated (e.g. by inserting a new event occurrence), the fluents' MVIs are calculated, and then stored for further use, allowing incremental computation for following updates. Also, every time a new event is added to the database, CEC manages to compute MVIs only for the fluents that can vary with that event, and does not check the MVIs of those fluents that cannot possibly change, thus avoiding unnecessary computation.

jREC is a reasoning tool based on Java and tuProlog that implements a lightweight version of CEC [5]. Since MAGPIE is also written in Java, it has been chosen to implement the proposed agent minds, in order to ensure seamless integration with the agent platform.

jREC consists of three main components:

- The Prolog theory, which represents the actual CEC axiomatization that is loaded into tuProlog;
- The Java engine, which allows to query and update the database without having to interact directly with tuProlog, as well as adding specific domain-dependent theories;
- The Tester, which is a GUI based stand-alone tool for editing theories, visualizing fluents' MVIs and event occurrences, mainly used for prototyping and developing domain-dependent theories.

2.3   Red-Black Trees

A red-black tree (RBT) is a well known data structure proposed by Rudolf Bayer in 1972 [3]. It is a binary search tree which provides $O(log(n))$ Worst Case time complexity for operations such as node searching, insertion and deletion, as well as $O(n)$ Worst Case space complexity [3]. This is made possible thanks to node coloring: every node of the tree is augmented with an extra bit, and based on the value of such bit, the node is considered to be red or black.

The aforementioned operations rely on such coloring feature to achieve Worst Case logarithmic time complexity and linear space complexity. In fact, every operation that modifies the RBT has to comply with very precise policies which constrain how the nodes should be moved or re-painted. These policies guarantees that the nodes in an RBT are always balanced after every operation, giving such data structure the property of self-balancing. Even though the obtained balance is not perfect, it is proven to be good enough to provide the declared performances [3].

Red-black trees can be effectively exploited as indexing data structures. As it will be also explained in Sect. 3, one of the agent minds that are proposed in this work relies on such RBT-based indexing in order to efficiently process event streams.

3   System Overview

The implemented agent minds run in Tier-2 of the MAGPIE agent-based PHS for self monitoring of diabetes. The entire PHS is depicted in Fig. 1. Each patient has its own agent composed by a body and a mind running on the personal server: in Tier-1 data are collected from the patients through a BAN; in Tier-2, the agent minds are responsible to trigger possible alerts based on the patients' physiological values, running domain dependent rules which could be customized for each patient. The triggered alerts have to be sent as a notification to medical doctors connected to Tier-3.

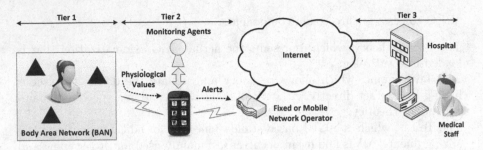

Fig. 1. The agentified PHS. The agent mind runs in Tier-2, to monitor the patient's physiological values.

3.1 MAGPIE Agent Platform

MAGPIE is an agent platform integrated with the Android OS. It plays the role of Tier-2 in a PHS by connecting the patient and the medical doctor, with the aim of improving the management of chronic diseases. From the side of the patient it collects physiological values, whereas from the medical side it models the medical knowledge in terms of monitoring rules expressed as domain dependent axioms of EC. Interested readers can find in [9] a description of the MAGPIE architecture and its integration with Android. In relation to this work, a monitoring rule is defined as a combination of events that trigger an alert to be reported to a medical doctor, where an event is considered as the measurement of a physiological parameter. Therefore, the following two types of monitoring rules are specified:

- Complex rules: consist of the combination of two or more events in a specific time window, where the order in which the events happen is not considered.
- Sequential rules: consist of the sequence of two or more events in a specific time window, where the particular order in which the events occur matters.

3.2 Diabetes Monitoring Rules

In order to detect alert conditions related to diabetes, a sequential and a complex rule patterns are proposed. These rule patterns are based on the literature available for glucose and blood pressure monitoring [6,16] and checks physiological values collected by the patient's BAN. The patterns identify alert conditions in the patient's health status by modeling the sensor inputs as events that are evaluated in the body of the rules. The two patterns are:

Pattern 1: Brittle diabetes, defined as a glucose rebound going from less than 3.8 mmol/l to more than 8.0 mmol/l in a period of six hours. This pattern can be expressed by a sequential rule.

Pattern 2: Pre-hypertension, defined as two events of high blood pressure in a period of one week. This pattern can be expressed by a complex rule.

Pattern 1 is implemented as follows:

$$initiatesAt(F = A, T) : -$$
$$happensAt(ev(2, A, W), T),$$
$$happensAt(ev(1, A, \_), T_1),$$
$$T_s \text{ is } (T - W),$$
$$T > T_1,$$
$$T_1 >= T_s,$$
$$no\_alert(A, T_s). \tag{9a}$$

$$terminatesAt(F = A, T) : -$$
$$happensAt(ev(1, A, \_), T). \tag{9b}$$

$$happensAt(ev(1, \text{'brittle diabetes'}, W), T) : -$$
$$hours\_to\_epoch(6, W),$$
$$happensAt(glucose(G), T),$$
$$G =< 3.8. \tag{9c}$$

$$happensAt(ev(2, \text{'brittle diabetes'}, W), T) : -$$
$$hours\_to\_epoch(6, W),$$
$$happensAt(glucose(G), T),$$
$$G >= 8. \tag{9d}$$

Rules (9a) and (9b) represent a generic sequential rule template with two events. In particular, the fluent F (i.e. the alert) is initiated with value A when: (i) two temporal ordered events occur inside a certain time window and (ii) when the fluent does not hold anywhere else inside the time window (no_alert/2). The fluent F is instead terminated when the first event of the ordering happens.

Rules (9c) and (9d) customize the template for the glucose monitoring use case. They instantiate the variables in the ev/3 term, specifying the time window width (W), the alert name (A) and the threshold values for G.

Pattern 2 is expressed in the following way:

$$initiatesAt(F = A, T) : -$$
$$happensAt(alertcheck(A, W, NMax_1), T),$$
$$T_s \text{ is } (T - W),$$
$$count\_events\_tw(N_1, evc(1, A), T_s, T),$$
$$N_1 >= NMax_1,$$
$$no\_alert(A, T_s). \tag{10a}$$

$$terminatesAt(F = A, T) : -$$
$$happensAt(alertcheck(A, W, \_), T),$$
$$holdsAt(F = A, T). \tag{10b}$$

$$\text{happensAt}(\text{evc}(1, \text{`pre-hypertension'}), T) : -$$
$$\text{happensAt}(\text{blood\_pressure}(S, D), T),$$
$$S >= 130,$$
$$D >= 80.$$

(10c)

$$\text{happensAt}(\text{alertcheck}(\text{`pre-hypertension'}, W, 2), T) : -$$
$$\text{weeks\_to\_epoch}(1, W),$$
$$\text{happensAt}(\text{evc}(1, \text{`pre-hypertension'}), T).$$

(10d)

Rules (10a) and (10b) represent a generic complex rule template with one event type. In particular, the fluent F (i.e. the alert) is initiated with value A when: (i) there are least $NMax_1$ occurrences of the alertcheck/3 event inside the time window and (ii) when the fluent does not hold anywhere else inside the time window (no_alert/2). Also, the count_events_tw/4 predicate is necessary to handle different event temporal orderings without having to duplicate the rule body for every permutation. Rules (10c) and (10d) customize the template for the hypertension monitoring use case. They instantiate the variables of the evc/2 and the alertcheck/3 terms specifying the time window width (W), the alert name (A) and the threshold values for S and D.

3.3   Event Handling with jREC

Efficient handling of massive event streams, while preserving the philosophy of Event Calculus, and in broader terms, of Logic Programming, is a non-trivial task. Techniques such as (i) event windowing/forgetting [1], (ii) theory precompilation [1] and (iii) a priori assumptions on event temporal ordering, can help to ease the burden of this process, but at the same time their adoption will cause the reasoning approach to be less general and less flexible. Therefore, since in real case monitoring scenarios these techniques and assumptions might simply not be applicable, finding alternatives ways to tackle the problem in a more general case becomes mandatory.

For example, jREC does not apply any simplifying assumption or technique to the event streams: this forces the reasoner to spend a very high amount of resources every time the engine's knowledge base (KB) is updated with new events. Whenever a list of new events has to be asserted into the KB, jREC must perform the following steps:

- Sort the list of new events chronologically;
- Read all the events already present in the KB and put them in a list;
- Retract all the events from the KB;
- Sort the list of KB's events chronologically;
- Merge the list of new events with the list of events read from the KB;
- Sort the newly obtained list chronologically and remove duplicates;
- Assert the events from the newly obtained list back into the KB;
- Calculate the effects on fluents' MVIs.

This procedure indeed maintains the reasoning as general and flexible as possible, but it is also the main source of jREC inefficiency, since every new event(s) insertion causes the engine to sort the event lists multiple times.

To tackle such issue, this paper proposes the integration of jREC with an indexing data structure, i.e. the previously mentioned red-black trees. RBTs will take the duty of maintaining the events temporal ordering by avoiding unnecessary sorting operations, and ensuring fast execution times.

The introduction of event indexing with RBTs allows to more precisely define the proposed agent minds:

- An agent mind based on the standard jREC implementation (standard jREC);
- An agent mind based on a custom jREC implementation, which has been augmented with RBT event indexing (RBT-index jREC).

It should be noticed that, since (i) an event normally contains multi-dimensional data (i.e. timestamp and physiological values), (ii) an RBT only allows single-dimensional indexing, and (iii) jREC needs the events to be ordered chronologically, the only choice is to consider the events timestamp as the key on which the indexing will be performed.

4 Test Setup and Results

The performances of the two jREC agent minds have been evaluated using the sequential and complex rule patterns described above. To accomplish that, synthetic datasets containing glucose and blood pressure measurements have been created. Each measurement is a tuple containing the value(s) and its timestamp.

4.1 Testing Protocol

To see how the performances of the agent minds evolve when the number of events increases, a series of random dataset has been created, each one containing a different number of events.

The events of each dataset are fed into the agent minds one by one, and the time needed by each agent to trigger the alert is recorded. Every experiment is repeated one-hundred times to obtain the mean and standard deviation values.

Due to the early stage of the work, the use of synthetic datasets did not represent a threat to the experiment validity. It instead turned out to be a useful feature, since it allowed to stress the agent minds on very specific and critical tasks.

4.2 Results and Discussion

The tests have been executed on an i7-6700K@4.20 GHz CPU with 16 GB@2400 MHz DDR4 RAM, running Ubuntu/Linux 16.04 and Java Runtime Environment 8u121.

It should be noticed that the main results of these tests are the execution time trends, rather than the absolute values themselves (since they vary with different machines).

From the plots in Fig. 2a and b, it is clear that the two agent minds show a very different behaviour: the execution time of the standard jREC agent mind grows in a polynomial fashion, and is considerably higher than the counterpart's. In fact, from the plots in Fig. 3a and b it can be observed that the execution time of the RBT-index jREC agent mind follows a logarithmic-like curve.

The polynomial trend exhibited by the standard jREC agent mind can be explained in terms of nested sortings: in fact, every time the engine knowledge base is updated with one or more events, the logic machinery of the engine launches multiple nested sorting clauses (see also Sect. 3.3).

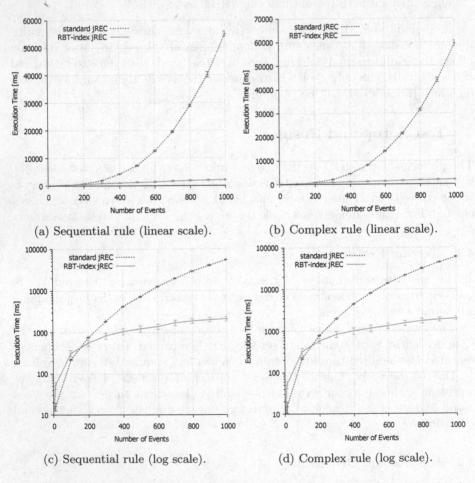

(a) Sequential rule (linear scale).   (b) Complex rule (linear scale).

(c) Sequential rule (log scale).   (d) Complex rule (log scale).

Fig. 2. Milliseconds needed by the two jREC agent minds to compute an alert, for the different rules.

On the other hand, the logarithmic-like trend of the RBT-index jREC agent mind highlight a direct correlation with the expected performance of the RBT-based indexing. It also demonstrates that, as the number of event grows, the execution time introduced by the reasoning on such events plays a minor role on the overall execution time. This can be explained by considering that the average number of events falling inside a rule time window is constant, since (i) the average event inter-arrival time and (ii) rules time-windows duration are fixed.

As a last remark on the performance gap, the logarithmic plots in Fig. 2c and d clearly highlight that, after 1000 events, the improvement almost reaches 2 orders of magnitude.

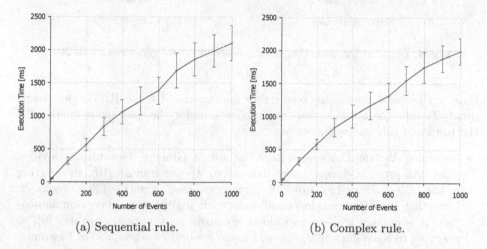

(a) Sequential rule.   (b) Complex rule.

Fig. 3. Detail of Fig. 2a and b, showing only RBT-index jREC agent mind's trends.

The execution times of the two agent minds in a scenario with a small number of events highlights some peculiar behaviours. As can be clearly seen from the plots (Fig. 4a and b), when the number of events is smaller than 100, the standard jREC agent mind shows better performances than the other. When the number of events reaches 200, the situation is the opposite, with the RBT-index agent mind being on top. This effect is due to the additional overhead in RBT-index agent mind: to be more precise, with very few events, the event-handling time gain obtained with the exploitation of the RBT-based indexing is not enough to compensate the additional overhead introduced by such data structure. By increasing the number of events, the event-handling time gain becomes increasingly more predominant over the data structure overhead, allowing the RBT-index jREC agent mind to perform better on massive event streams.

With the machine used for the tests, it is shown that the RBT-index jREC agent mind exhibits a clear performance improvement over the standard jREC agent mind. The execution time trends suggest that even scenarios with more

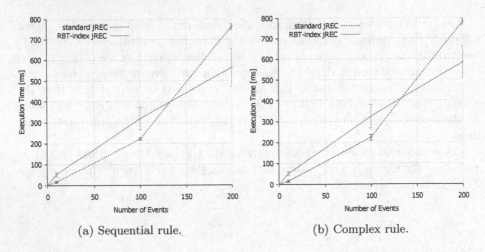

(a) Sequential rule.   (b) Complex rule.

Fig. 4. Detail of Fig. 2a and b, with number of events going from 0 to 200.

than a thousand events are reasonably manageable by the RBT-index agent mind. Thus, some possible real-case applications for the said agent mind, with the proposed rule patterns, can be:

- Detecting Brittle Diabetes with Continuous Glucose Monitoring devices. They can provide glucose measurements up to one minute [16], so referring to the Rule Pattern 1, it would mean a worst case scenario of 360 events.
- Detecting Pre-Hypertension conditions with digital arm sphygmomanometers. It is enough to have two blood pressure measurements per day [6], so referring to Rule Pattern 2, it would mean a worst case scenario of 14 events.

Even though the standard jREC agent mind performs slightly better with a low number of events, this is not enough to justify its usage only in such scenario.

5   Related Work

Multi-Agent Systems (MASs) meet the requirements of the healthcare sector: context awareness, reliability, data abstraction and interoperability, unobtrusiveness [4]. From a requirements engineering perspective, goal-oriented and agent-based design methodologies are useful to tailor pervasive systems to end-users and stakeholders' needs [11]. When applied to PHSs, agent-based modeling has the potential to bring the decision making at the level of self-management of chronic diseases [21]. In the implementation phase, MASs in PHSs pursue the enhancement of home-based self-care by using networks of sensors and remote assistance, to increase the satisfaction of the patient and make an efficient use of resources [17].

Reasoning agents in PHSs allow to transfer part of the knowledge from domain experts to the handheld devices used to perform the self-management of chronic diseases. Beyond PHSs, other applications include energy management [25], to control energy demand and production, home automation [26], to coordinate the available appliances, and ambient assisted living [23,27], with monitoring purposes. In the context of PHSs, EC and MASs have been successfully applied to the self-management of diabetes [7,19]. However, such works do not take into account the scalability of the PHS. In fact, a clear advantage of reasoning agents in the Tier-2 of PHSs is the system scalability with increasing number of patients, as showed in [8]. Nevertheless, in such research, the scalability of the agent minds with high streams of events is not considered. Thus, there is the need to find the suitable tools to implement agent minds, which are supposed to run in portable devices, even with high numbers of events and large datasets. This is especially true for EC given its complexity. Indeed, non-logic based pattern recognition has been proved, overall, more efficient than traditional EC when performing predictions. However, it lacks the potential of coding domain experts' knowledge into logic rules and needs to train on large amounts of data. Hence, caching and windowing techniques to make EC efficient and applicable with large scale dataset have been investigated [1,5]. There are some already available tools that allow logic programming in terms of EC. One of such is DECReasoner [22], a Discrete Event Calculus Reasoner: it implements EC without any caching mechanism and, thus, it is not usable for this research, due to its computation time with the datasets used for the performance tests. A more efficient EC implementation is RTEC, which adds to EC support for handling event streams [1]. However, RTEC techniques such as event windowing and theory pre-compilation do not match the flexibility requirements (i.e. editing agent's theories at runtime) of the proposed PHS. In addition, it is not compatible with the platform, as the agent-oriented PHS is based on tuProlog and Java [8]. Thus, jREC has been used to implement a prototype for the proposed agent mind, since it implements Cached Event Calculus [5] with tuProlog, a Java-based Prolog engine [15]. Moreover, being Java-based, jREC and tuProlog can run on Android devices, allowing to run the proposed agent mind on handheld devices.

6   Conclusions

In this work, two rule-based minds for monitoring agents running on Tier-2 of a PHS have been presented and tested. Being both integrated into the MAGPIE agent platform, one is based on the plain jREC reasoner and the other is a customization of the standard jREC reasoner augmented with an RBT-based indexing technique. In order to be used in real monitoring scenarios, the agent minds have to be able to process massive event streams, represented by the patient's physiological values. Therefore, in addition to the customization of the jREC reasoning engine, the main contribution of this paper is the performance evaluation of proposed agent minds on the time needed to trigger alerts based on glucose and blood pressure levels, in a diabetes monitoring scenario. Two real application scenarios for the proposed agent minds are the detection of brittle diabetes, with Continuous Glucose Monitoring, and the detection of Pre-Hypertension conditions, with devices such as digital arm sphygmomanometers.

As future work, since PHSs are intended for the self-management of diabetes with handheld devices, the tests should be performed on mobile phones, to obtain more realistic figures. In this direction, the performance of the RBT-index jREC agent mind can be further enhanced by improving the current indexing solution. Furthermore, in order to validate the usefulness of the rules, the tests should run on real datasets. Lastly, the system can be applied to other use cases, in order to model rules for other diseases.

References

1. Artikis, A., Sergot, M., Paliouras, G.: An event calculus for event recognition. IEEE Trans. Knowl. Data Eng. **27**(4), 895–908 (2015)
2. Bauer, U.E., Briss, P.A., Goodman, R.A., Bowman, B.A.: Prevention of chronic disease in the 21st century: elimination of the leading preventable causes of premature death and disability in the USA. Lancet **384**(9937), 45–52 (2014)
3. Bayer, R.: Symmetric binary b-trees: data structure and maintenance algorithms. Acta Informatica **1**(4), 290–306 (1972). https://doi.org/10.1007/BF00289509
4. Bergenti, F., Poggi, A.: Multi-agent systems for e-health: recent projects and initiatives. In: 10th Workshop on Objects and Agents (WOA 2009) (2009)
5. Bragaglia, S., Chesani, F., Mello, P., Montali, M., Torroni, P.: Reactive event calculus for monitoring global computing applications. In: Artikis, A., Craven, R., Kesim Çiçekli, N., Sadighi, B., Stathis, K. (eds.) Logic Programs, Norms and Action. LNCS (LNAI), vol. 7360, pp. 123–146. Springer, Heidelberg (2012). https://doi.org/10.1007/978-3-642-29414-3_8
6. British Hypertension Society: Home blood pressure monitoring protocol, February 2017. http://www.bhsoc.org/files/4414/1088/8031/Protocol.pdf
7. Bromuri, S., Puricel, S., Schumann, R., Krampf, J., Ruiz, J., Schumacher, M.: An expert personal health system to monitor patients affected by gestational diabetes mellitus: a feasibility study. J. Ambient Intell. Smart Environ. **8**(2), 219–237 (2016)
8. Brugués, A., Bromuri, S., Barry, M., del Toro, O.J., Mazurkiewicz, M.R., Kardas, P., Pegueroles, J., Schumacher, M.: Processing diabetes mellitus composite events in MAGPIE. J. Med. Syst. **40**(2), 44 (2016)
9. Brugués, A., Bromuri, S., Pegueroles-Valles, J., Schumacher, M.I.: MAGPIE: an agent platform for the development of mobile applications for pervasive healthcare. In: Proceedings of the 3rd International Workshop on Artificial Intelligence and Assistive Medicine (AI-AM/NetMed), pp. 6–10 (2014)
10. Calvaresi, D., Cesarini, D., Marinoni, M., Buonocunto, P., Bandinelli, S., Buttazzo, G.: Non-intrusive patient monitoring for supporting general practitioners in following diseases evolution. In: Ortuño, F., Rojas, I. (eds.) IWBBIO 2015. LNCS, vol. 9044, pp. 491–501. Springer, Cham (2015). https://doi.org/10.1007/978-3-319-16480-9_48
11. Calvaresi, D., Cesarini, D., Sernani, P., Marinoni, M., Dragoni, A.F., Sturm, A.: Exploring the ambient assisted living domain: a systematic review. J. Ambient Intell. Hum. Comput. **8**, 1–19 (2016)
12. Calvaresi, D., Marinoni, M., Sturm, A., Schumacher, M., Buttazzo, G.: The challenge of real-time multi-agent systems for enabling IoT and CPS. In: Proceedings of IEEE/WIC/ACM International Conference on Web Intelligence (WI 2017) (2017)

13. Calvaresi, D., Schumacher, M., Marinoni, M., Hilfiker, R., Dragoni, A.F., Buttazzo, G.: Agent-based systems for telerehabilitation: strengths, limitations and future challenges. In: Proceedings of the 10th Workshop on Agents Applied in Health Care (A2HC 2017) (2017)
14. Chittaro, L., Montanari, A.: Efficient temporal reasoning in the cached event calculus. Comput. Intell. **12**(3), 359–382 (1996). http://dx.doi.org/10.1111/j.1467-8640.1996.tb00267.x
15. Denti, E., Omicini, A., Ricci, A.: Multi-paradigm Java-Prolog integration in tuProlog. Sci. Comput. Program. **57**(2), 217–250 (2005)
16. Dungan, K.: Monitoring technologies - continuous glucose monitoring, mobile technology, biomarkers of glycemic control. In: De Groot, L.J., Beck-Peccoz, P., Chrousos, G., Dungan, K., Grossman, A., Hershman, J.M., Singer, F. (eds.) Endotext [Internet] (2014)
17. Isern, D., Moreno, A.: A systematic literature review of agents applied in healthcare. J. Med. Syst. **40**(2), 43 (2015)
18. Isern, D., Sánchez, D., Moreno, A.: Agents applied in health care: a review. Int. J. Med. Inform. **79**(3), 145–166 (2010)
19. Kafalı, Ö., Bromuri, S., Sindlar, M., van der Weide, T., Aguilar Pelaez, E., Schaechtle, U., Alves, B., Zufferey, D., Rodriguez-Villegas, E., Schumacher, M.I., et al.: Commodity12: a smart e-health environment for diabetes management. J. Ambient Intell. Smart Environ. **5**(5), 479–502 (2013)
20. Kowalski, R., Sergot, M.: A logic-based calculus of events. New Gener. Comput. **4**(1), 67–95 (1986)
21. Montagna, S., Omicini, A., Angeli, F.D., Donati, M.: Towards the adoption of agent-based modelling and simulation in mobile health systems for the self-management of chronic diseases. In: Proceedings of the 17th Workshop "From Objects to Agents", Catania, Italy, 29–30 July 2016, pp. 100–105 (2016)
22. Mueller, E.T.: Commonsense Reasoning: An Event Calculus Based Approach, 2nd edn. Morgan Kaufmann Publishers Inc., San Francisco (2015)
23. Nefti, S., Manzoor, U., Manzoor, S.: Cognitive agent based intelligent warning system to monitor patients suffering from dementia using ambient assisted living. In: 2010 International Conference on Information Society, pp. 92–97 (2010)
24. Peine, A., Moors, E.H.: Valuing health technology - habilitating and prosthetic strategies in personal health systems. Technol. Forecast. Soc. Change **93**, 68–81 (2015)
25. Ramchurn, S.D., Vytelingum, P., Rogers, A., Jennings, N.: Agent-based control for decentralised demand side management in the smart grid. In: The 10th International Conference on Autonomous Agents and Multiagent Systems, vol. 1, pp. 5–12 (2011)
26. Ruta, M., Scioscia, F., Loseto, G., Sciascio, E.D.: Semantic-based resource discovery and orchestration in home and building automation: a multi-agent approach. IEEE Trans. Industr. Inf. **10**(1), 730–741 (2014)
27. Sernani, P., Claudi, A., Dragoni, A.: Combining artificial intelligence and netmedicine for ambient assisted living: a distributed BDI-based expert system. Int. J. EHealth Med. Commun. **6**(4), 62–76 (2015)
28. Silverman, B.G., Hanrahan, N., Bharathy, G., Gordon, K., Johnson, D.: A systems approach to healthcare: agent-based modeling, community mental health, and population well-being. Artif. Intell. Med. **63**(2), 61–71 (2015)
29. Tartarisco, G., Baldus, G., Corda, D., Raso, R., Arnao, A., Ferro, M., Gaggioli, A., Pioggia, G.: Personal health system architecture for stress monitoring and support to clinical decisions. Comput. Commun. **35**(11), 1296–1305 (2012)

30. Touati, F., Tabish, R.: U-healthcare system: state-of-the-art review and challenges. J. Med. Syst. **37**(3), 9949 (2013)
31. Varshney, U.: Pervasive healthcare and wireless health monitoring. Mob. Netw. Appl. **12**(2–3), 113–127 (2007)
32. Global Report on Diabetes. World Health Organization, Geneva (2016)
33. Zimmet, P., Alberti, K.G., Magliano, D.J., Bennett, P.H.: Diabetes mellitus statistics on prevalence and mortality: facts and fallacies. Nature Rev. Endocrinol. **12**(10), 616–622 (2016)

Personal Assistant Agents in Health-Care

A Personal Medical Digital Assistant Agent for Supporting Human Operators in Emergency Scenarios

Angelo Croatti$^{(\boxtimes)}$ ⓘ, Sara Montagna ⓘ, and Alessandro Ricci ⓘ

DISI, University of Bologna, Via Sacchi 3, Cesena, Italy
{a.croatti,sara.montagna,a.ricci}@unibo.it

Abstract. In this paper we present Trauma Tracker, a project – in cooperation with the Trauma Center of a hospital in Italy – in which agent technologies are exploited to realise Personal Medical Digital Assistant Agents (PMDA) supporting a Trauma Team in trauma management operations. This project aims at exploring the fruitful integration of software personal agents with wearable/eyewear computing, based on mobile and wearable devices such as smart-glasses. The key functionality of Trauma Tracker is to keep track of relevant events occurring during the management of a trauma, for different purposes. The basic one – discussed in detail in this paper – is to have an accurate documentation of the trauma, to automate the creation (and management) of reports and to enable offline data analysis, useful for performance evaluation and to improve the work of the Trauma Team. Then, tracking is essential to conceive more involved assisting functionalities by the PMDA, from monitoring and warning generation to suggesting actions to perform—fully exploiting the hands-free interface of wearable technologies. This goes towards the idea – envisioned in the paper – of *augmented physicians* working in *augmented hospitals*, in which software personal agents are exploited along with enabling technologies from wearable and pervasive computing, augmented reality, to create novel smart environments to support individual and cooperative work of healthcare professionals.

1 Introduction

In the last decade, information and communication technologies (ICT) witnessed an impressive progress, in particular mobile and *wearable* ones, making the visions about pervasive computing in hospitals [2,27,48] more and more a reality. Nowadays Personal Digital Assistants (PDA) and tablets are widely deployed in various healthcare contexts [18]. Modern smartphones are powerful computing devices, featuring a variety of onboard sensors (camera, GPS, NFC reader, ...), a robust support for pervasive interaction with an ecosystem of Bluetooth-enabled external devices and wireless networking. This makes it possible to design complex mobile computing applications, eventually interacting with services in local area networks and on the Internet/cloud.

© Springer International Publishing AG 2017
S. Montagna et al. (Eds.): A2HC 2017/A-HEALTH 2017, LNAI 10685, pp. 59–75, 2017.
https://doi.org/10.1007/978-3-319-70887-4_4

Besides mobile computing, technologies for *wearable computing* [20] and *eye-wear computing* [5] are achieving a level of maturity that makes it possible to exploit them out of labs, in real-world professional contexts. In particular, smart-glass technologies – e.g., Vuzix m300, Epson Moverio BT-200, Microsoft Hololens – allow to designing a new generation of (pervasive) software systems exploiting different degrees of Mixed and Augmented Reality [43]. These devices are basic bricks to realise *hands-free* or *use-on-the-go* systems [40,41], in which users can, e.g., asynchronously perceive information, data generated by the application without the need of changing the focus of their current activity and limiting as much as possible the use of hands to act/interact with the device.

The development of these technologies allows for devising new kind of *software personal agents*, assisting healthcare professionals in doing their job. In this paper we refer to this agent technology as Personal Medical Digital Assistant agent (PMDA). A main healthcare context where this kind of technology can be useful is the *emergency*. In this context, agent technologies have been already proposed e.g. for emergency coordination.

In this paper, we present and discuss a further novel case, concerning the development of a PMDA for *trauma documentation and management*. The project – called Trauma Tracker – is being developed in cooperation with the Emergency Department, a Trauma Center, of a hospital in Italy. The first prototype of Trauma Tracker has been implemented using BDI-based (Belief-Desire-Intention) agent technologies—a version of the JaCaMo platform [3] running on Android-based mobile and wearable devices.

Trauma Tracker has been designed in a modular way, to support increasing levels of functionalities and services. The base level concerns tracking events and data, for documentation purposes—which is the focus of this paper. A first validation of the system has been carried on by the trauma team, remarking both the benefits with respect to the current practice, and current limits, providing feedbacks for further development of the system. Upper levels concern functionalities more oriented to real-time *assistance*, from the reactive generation of warnings to more proactive form of assistance (e.g., suggesting the actions to perform), exploiting the hands-free capabilities of wearable technologies such as the smart-glasses. This goes towards the vision of *augmented physicians* working in *augmented hospitals*, in which software personal agents are exploited along with enabling technologies from wearable and pervasive computing, and augmented reality, to create novel PMDA and smart environments for assisting healthcare professionals.

The remainder of the paper is organised as follows. In Sect. 2 we provide a background and overview on related work about agent technologies applied to emergency. After that, in Sect. 3 we introduce the Trauma Tracker project, the levels of support which is meant to provide and its coarse-grained architecture, including – as a key component – the PMDA. Then, in Sect. 4, we discuss in detail the *Tracking Level* of Trauma Tracker, which is the one developed to tackle the trauma documentation problem. In particular, we discuss in the design and prototype implementation of the PMDA using JaCaMo and a first evaluation. After that, in Sect. 5 we discuss the level of assistance that we aim at building on top of the tracking level, envisioning the idea of *augmented physicians* working in *augmented hospitals*. Finally, in Sect. 6 we draw some conclusions, briefly depicting our ongoing and future work.

2 Agents in Heathcare Emergency Scenarios

The unquestioned benefit of the introduction of ICT into healthcare systems is already recognised worldwide since ICT successfully addresses the vast set of characteristics and situations proper of the healthcare scenario —such as mobility, time-critical, distribution and large-scale coordination, context-awareness, decision-making, interoperability, complexity. Last-generation ICT infrastructures and services, especially the emergence of wearable and mobile technologies, opened new frontiers in healthcare by efficaciously supplying the work of hospital staff, doctors, and patients. The so-called *e-Health* [52] and *m-Health* [38] improved the quality of health-services, providing technologies for different purposes, such as acquiring and sharing patient data through Electronic Medical Records (EMR), automating administrative health-related processes, providing telemedicine services, remote and mobile monitoring, and much more [28,50].

In particular, the adoption of the agent paradigm seems to be particularly suited to improve the performance of an ICT infrastructure in terms of interoperability, scalability and reconfigurability. Literature refers a wide range of applications of the agent framework in e-Health for different purposes. A comprehensive review is provided in [15], where the main categories of applications identified are: *(i)* Medical data management: accessing, integrating and sharing patient' data from different remote sources is crucial for easing the work of physicians and for statistical analysis purposes [28,49]; *(ii)* Decision support systems: supporting physicians in their fast-paced work can reduce human errors, and safe time [6]; *(iii)* Planning and resource allocation: scheduling decisions on the allocation of professional and physical resources must be coordinated by planning techniques [46]; *(iv)* Remote care: mainly devoted to remote patient monitoring, it allows on one side patients with reduced mobility to not travel towards healthcare facilities for vital signs check-up, on the other side physicians to observe the dynamic of the patient's health and provide opportune recommendations tailored to the patient [44]. Moreover, the literature proposes the development of agent systems for *chronic diseases management*, such as diabetes, respiratory illnesses, and cardiovascular diseases [36]. The goal is to develop applications enabling a shift of the control of chronic illness from the caregiver to the patients themselves, namely the *self-management* of chronic diseases [23]. In this context an agent-based platform enables: *healthcare professionals* to be continuously updated on the patient's health by receiving data such as vital signs measures decreasing the occasions for patients to travel to health facilities; *patients* to be supported in daily decisions by instructions delivered by the application that is based on the elaboration of such data.

In this paper, we discuss specific issues related to the Emergency Department (ED), that is one of the most critical and challenging hospital departments, since it requires reactivity, quick and coordinated response, fast-paced and accurate decision-making. In this scenario, there are three key issues that may be tackled by the agent technology. First of all, the fast-paced sequence of events during a trauma resuscitation leaves little time for physicians to reason about the best treatment and care. A PMDA can thus support human operators by autonomously providing suggestions on the best choice. This would reduce human errors while saving time and increasing team performance. Secondly, an accurate documentation of trauma resuscitation seems to be crucial to improve the quality of trauma care where, according to [14] "Quality of trauma care can be defined as achieving the best possible outcome for a given set of clinical circumstances". Third, agent technologies – in particular Multi-Agent Systems – can be exploited to support the coordination among the various actors involved in the trauma management. An example is presented in [10], about the Ubimedic2 agent framework for supporting rescue operations. [28] presents CASCOM, a distributed multi-agent system for the execution of smart emergencies by providing efficient remote healthcare in case of unexpected events. Within the platform distributed data and information can be retrieved and make available to physicians everywhere, thus enabling easier and faster choices.

The trauma tracker project focuses on the first two issues. The PMDA is a *software personal agent* assisting the activity of the Trauma Team. Personal assistants are a well-known application of software agents [19,21,25]. Existing proposal and technologies have been developed for different kind of purposes and capabilities, from scheduling joint activities [22,37,51], monitoring and reminding users of key timepoints [7,47], sharing information, assisting in negotiation decision support [17]. Compared to SPAs discussed in literature, the PMDA in our project have two main specific coarse-grained features:

- the kind of assistances requires the continuous observation of both the dynamic state of the context where the physician is acting, and also what specifically the physician is *doing* and *perceiving* in that context;
- to be able to provide assistance while the physician is carrying on her practical activity, *without distracting or interrupting her action*.

From a technological point of view, the design of these agents can benefit from the availability of wearable technologies such as smart-glasses, and, more generally, from the fruitful interaction with the research developed in the context of wearable and eyewear computing [5].

3   The Trauma Tracker Project

Trauma Tracker has been conceived and designed by taking in consideration the structure and work organisation of the Trauma Team. The team leader – the so called *Trauma Leader*, usually a senior official – is in charge of producing the documentation paper. However this is just one of the several functions she/he has.

During trauma resuscitation Trauma Leaders supervise the work of their teams and are actively involved in the actual resuscitation, and only *after* that work is finished they produce the report. That is, they recall and write down in prose the main facts of the trauma resuscitation process, documenting from memory and not real-time. This is the typical situation of hospital emergency departments in Italy—besides the specific trauma center considered in this paper. Therefore, in this case, the availability of a system based on mobile and wearable technologies for trauma tracking and assistance, not only would improve the accuracy of the trauma documentation, but also significantly reduce the cognitive burden of the trauma team – of the Trauma Leader in particular – to create the reports. Nevertheless, such a system is useful also when a *scribe* or *recorder* is available in the Trauma Team, usually a nurse, like it happens in hospitals in Europe and US—to support her work.

3.1 Levels of Support

The Trauma Tracker project has a twofold general objective. A short-term one is enabling a systematically and as-much-as possible seamlessly tracking all the trauma managed in the Trauma Center, to increase both the quality and quantity of the collected data and to provide a flexible and comprehensive way to manage and analyse such data, structured in reports. This is the job of the Tracking Level, which is the base level of Trauma Tracker. The design and prototype development of this level, as well as its first validation, will be discussed in Sect. 4.

A medium-term one is to introduce different kind of *assistance* to support the Trauma Team during the management of a trauma. Such assistance ranges from monitoring to suggesting. This level will be discussed in Sect. 5.

3.2 Coarse-Grained Architecture

The coarse-grained general architecture of TraumaTracker, represented in Fig. 1, is agent and service oriented, and includes four main parts:

- The PMDA, referred as *Trauma Assistant Agent*.
- a set of Web-based services deployed in the hospital local area network, referred as GT^2 *infrastructure*.
- a set of pervasive services, provided by devices deployed in the physical environment of the hospital, referred as GT^2 *pervasive*.
- a set of Web-apps, enabling users to access and interact with some of the GT^2 *infrastructure* services, referred as GT^2 *apps*.

The *Trauma Assistant Agent* runs on the mobile (a tablet) and wearable (smart-glasses) used by the Trauma Leader. It interacts with the services of the GT^2 *infrastructure* and GT^2 *pervasive*. The GT^2 *infrastructure* includes a set of web services that are exploited by the *Trauma Assistant Agent* and by the web-apps. The GT^2 *pervasive* currently includes a set of beacons placed in all rooms

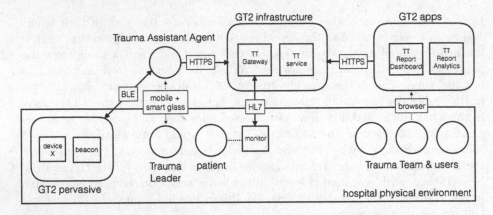

Fig. 1. Trauma tracker coarse-grained architecture.

involved in the management of a trauma, to enable the room-level localisation for the PMDA.

A specific set of services in GT^2 *infrastructure* and apps in GT^2 *apps* is available to support the functionalities of the levels identified above. Currently, these services include (1) the *TT Report Management Service* – that provides a REST-ful APIs for collecting and managing trauma reports and accessing to related statistical data – and (2) the *TT Vital Signs Monitor Service* – that provides APIs for dynamically retrieving the vital signs parameters of a patient under trauma, and services to realise continuous monitoring. Data collected by these services are made available to other hospital applications running on the same infrastructure, in an open ecosystem perspective. Finally, GT^2 *apps* currently includes a *TT Report Dashboard*, a web application that allows users – e.g., the member of the Trauma Team – to access the trauma documentation i.e. the reports, to manage, print and export them, as well as to do basic statistics.

In the next section we consider in detail the design and implementation of the Tracking Level, focusing in particular on the Trauma Assistant Agent.

4   The Tracking Level

The Tracking Level tackles the trauma documentation problem. In this section, we first discuss this problem in more detail, then we describe the design and implementation of the Trauma Tracker prototype, focusing in particular on the Trauma Assistant Agent, and finally we discuss its evaluation.

4.1   The Trauma Documentation Problem: Details

The documentation of a trauma, known in the literature as *trauma documentation,* is meant to be acquired during the process of trauma resuscitation, reporting where and when crucial events occurred, which and when treatments are given, procedures are performed, and finally it should report repeated vital signs measures. The documentation is crucial because it is used to make the most informed choice for patient medication and management, and later to evaluate the work of team members by producing data and statistics such as: time of team activation, primary assessment, arrival time of attending physician.

There reasons that make this task – i.e., producing an accurate documentation in the context of trauma resuscitation – challenging are manyfold [35]. First of all, trauma resuscitation is a fast-paced process, and very few time is left for documenting the process whilst some of the data to be documented are instead time-consuming. Secondly, multiple events happen simultaneously. To treat severe injuries, potentially life-threatening, team members perform concurrent tasks and parallel activities. Monitoring all of them is not trivial. Finally, the person in charge of documenting is often multitasking, his/her resources are not completely dedicated to the documentation task but he/she also performs other activities.

Nowadays most of the EDs adopt *handwritten paper records and flow sheets* for acquiring data [24,35]. The process of data acquisition is mainly conducted during the trauma resuscitation – or sometimes immediately after by collective memory and verbal communication – by the *recorder*, a person with that specific function. Papers are then sent to central bureau where data are manually entered from the sheets into a computerised databank. The overall procedure produces incomplete or even wrong documentation for two main reasons: (*i*) data acquisition is often inaccurate and crucial data are lacking. This is due to several reasons, some of which are due to the intrinsic characteristics of the context, as cited above: multitasking of the person in charge of acquiring data, parallel activities of the different members of the team, multiple data to be recorded, retrospective documenting from collective memory; (*ii*) manual transfer of data from paper to electronic format can introduce oversights. Furthermore, it is expensive in terms of time spent to complete the overall procedure and of workload.

The main objective of the Tracking Level of Trauma Tracker is then to help human operators – the Trauma Leader in particular – in producing an accurate trauma documentation, minimising as much as possible the human intervention and burden.

4.2   Trauma Assistant Agent Tasks

In the Tracking Level, the main tasks of the Trauma Assistant Agent are: (*i*) tracking events occurring in the emergency rooms related to a specific patient, inferring as much as possible data from the context (e.g., the place where a procedure is performed), and (*ii*) at the end of the trauma management, producing and sending a report to be sent to the *TT Report Management Service*.

Event tracking is mainly a reactive activity, in which the Trauma Assistant Agent:

- keeps track of the actions performed by the trauma team. These actions can be either procedures (e.g., endotracheal intubation, thoracic drainage, application of a tourniquet and many others) or drug/blood product infusion (e.g., millilitres of crystalloids or hypertonic solution, adrenaline, atropine, pools of cryoprecipitates, etc.);

– allows the trauma leader to take snapshots, record video or audio annotation, to be included in the report, exploiting the camera equipped with the smart-glasses;

– allows to retrieve, display and track the current value of patient's vital signs— by interacting with the *TT Vital Signs Monitor Service* service. These data must be automatically retrieved and annotated *(i)* when a procedure or the administration of a particular drug are performed; *(ii)* periodically, with a period that depends of the specific location of the patient in the emergency room (i.e. the period of vital signs monitoring could be different if the patient is currently in shock-room rather than in the TAC room).

Every event/note tracked by the agent includes both temporal (date and time) and spatial (location, specific room) information.

At the beginning of the trauma management, the system provides an easy-to-use form to annotate, in a qualitative way, the state of health in which the patient is (i.e. if his heart rate is normal rather than bradycardic or tachycardic, if the patient is breathing spontaneously or not, if external bleeding are present, and many others). Then, the system allows to annotate important variations to the patient vital signs (i.e. the patient that was hypoxic has returned to have a normal oxygen saturation). Finally, when the trauma management is completed, the Trauma Leader can annotate the final destination of the patient (i.e. emergency room observation area, ICU, mortuary). After that, the full report about

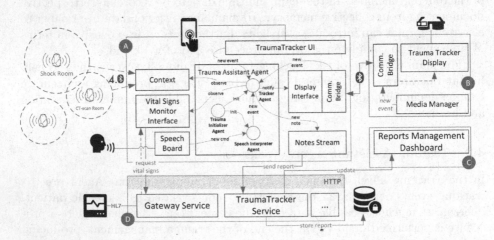

Fig. 2. Trauma Tracker system logical architecture. Parts (A) and (B) represent the Trauma Leader subsystem and in particular the Trauma Assistant Agent, Part (C) is the Reports Management subsystem and, finally, Part (D) represents the GT^2 infrastructure.

the trauma – including also photos, videos, vocal notes – is automatically sent and stored on a server, exploiting the hospital WiFi Local Area Network.

An important and challenging aspect of the agent is the strategy used to keep track of the actions performed on the patient by the trauma team. Currently, this occurs by reacting to commands that are explicitly requested by the Trauma Leader, either exploiting the user interface provided on the smartphone device where the agent is running, or as speech commands. The UI must be necessarily very simple and effective, minimizing the number of interactions and taps required to specify the action performed.

4.3 Design and Implementation

The Trauma Assistant Agent is designed upon the BDI (Belief-Desire-Intention) agent model/architecture. The BDI has been originally introduced to design real-time intelligent system assisting humans in critical operations [30], featuring the capability of integrating a goal-oriented behaviour – i.e., the agent has explicit goals to achieve and for that purpose it selects and executes plans – and a reactive behaviour – i.e., while executing the plans it can promptly react to events occurring in the environment, eventually executing further plans to handle them. This model/architecture makes it possible to easily design a Trauma Assistant Agent with the reactive capabilities required by the Tracking Level, yet being ready for designing and implementing more pro-active features required by the Assisting Level.

In BDI computational models/languages [29], such reactive capabilities can be effectively modelled in terms of a set of predefined *plans* that are triggered by events occurring in the environment. In our case, such events are about actions carried on by the Trauma Team on the patient, multi-media annotation requests by the Trauma Leader (snapshots, video, vocal notes), and events concerning changes of: Patient's vital parameters, the location (room) where the Trauma is taking place, the Trauma Team organisation (e.g., the change of the Trauma Leader).

Besides BDI, the A&A conceptual model [26] has been adopted to model and design the *agent environment*. This is useful to modularise the set of percepts and actions available to agents into dynamic modules called *artifacts*, which represents – from the agent point of view – resources and tools that can be used to do its job. In particular:

- a TraumaTracker UI artifact is used to collect and make observable to the Trauma Assistant Agent the stream of events about actions performed by the Trauma Team and requests from the Trauma Leader;
- a Display Interface artifact provides actions to display messages and information to be perceived by the Trauma Leader (either through the tablet or the smart-glasses);
- a Context artifact keep tracks and makes it observable the current location of the Trauma Leader (i.e., the room), exploiting a BLE beacon-based localisation infrastructure deployed in the hospital environment, part of the GT^2 *pervasive*;

– a Vital Signs Monitoring Interface artifact keeps track of and makes it observable the updated data about patient's vital signs, interacting with *TT Vital Signs Monitor Service* service.
– a Notes Stream artifact to persistently store the stream of notes carrying information about the events and providing other functionalities related to report generation and delivery to the *TT Report Management Service* service.

Figure 2 shows a sketch of the architecture of Trauma Tracker, with in evidence the agents and artifacts involved.

4.4   Prototype Implementation

The Trauma Assistant Agent has been implemented using JaCaMo, a BDI-based multi-agent oriented programming platform, which integrates the Jason agent programming language (to program BDI agents), the CArtAgO environment programming framework (to program agents' environment) and MOISE organization framework (to specify MAS organization) [3]. In particular, a version of JaCaMo running on mobile and wearable devices has been exploited, based on JaCa-Android [34], which introduces an agent-oriented programming model to design, develop and run agent-based applications on top of the Google Android platform.

Even if at the logical level the Trauma Assistant Agent is a single conceptual high-level agent, the implementation in JaCaMo includes multiple Jason agents that work together inside an environment composed of a set of resources and services wrapped inside a proper set of CArtAgO artifacts. In particular, current design includes three Jason agents (see Fig. 2, part A), each one in charge of a different task:

– The *Trauma Initializer Agent*, responsible for initializing the tracking phase and collecting (and store) all preliminary information, essential for reports creation, including the identity of the trauma leader and the patient's initial health status.
– The *Tracker Agent*, which is the core of the Trauma Assistant Agent, encapsulating most of its functionalities. This Jason agent is in charge of keeping track of the trauma events – by reacting to events generated by corresponding artifacts (TraumaTracker UI, Context and Vital Signs Monitoring Interface) – and of incrementally building the report and making the Trauma Leader aware of specific information when needed – by using actions provided by the other artifacts (Note Stream and Display Interface).
– The *Speech Interpreter Agent*, responsible for the interpretation of speech commands. In particular, this agent recognises if a particular command may be accepted in that particular instant of the trauma management process – according to the actions work-flow – and, if so, translate it into an appropriate event to be perceived by the Tracker Agent.

The full source code of the project is available on a public repository[1].

---

[1] https://bitbucket.org/pslabteam/traumatracker.

4.5 Evaluation

A first qualitative validation of the system has been carried on by the trauma team in a simulated environment, focusing in particular on the usability of the user interface (UI) and the responsiveness of the system. The basic configuration of the system – using the mobile devices only, without wearable technologies – appears to be ready and robust enough for being experimented in the real-world, providing already clear and measurable benefits – in terms of saved time and accuracy of the data – with respect to the current paper-based practice. So the next step, in this case, will be a further validation stage, in which the system is gradually introduced in the current practice, starting from the management of less critical trauma. Besides, this further stage will be essential to realise a more rigorous quantitative analysis and validation of the approach.

The adoption of smart-glasses – e.g., the intermediate configuration of the system – proved to be valuable to show information about vital signs in particular when the Trauma Leader is far from the vital signs monitor, and to take snapshots/video. As expected, the key benefit is to enable a first form of hands-free support, so that the Trauma Leader can take a snapshot or perceive information about the parameters without changing her focus and distracting from the scene. A critical point to be tackled before moving to the next validation stage is about the physical head mounting of the smart-glasses. On the one hand, current setting proved to be stable enough to deal with (abrupt) Trauma Leader's movements; on the other hand, we need to improve the flexibility in allowing the Trauma Leader to dynamically and seamlessly raise/drop the smart-glasses in some moments (to get them back, then), as well as reducing the effort (and time) needed to adjust the device.

Not surprisingly, the aspect that needs to be strongly improved in order to be usable in the trauma real-world settings is speech recognition. Currently, the performance is acceptable only for recognising basic commands used sporadically. This is not unexpected, since we are not using in the prototype specific speech recognition engine but the one available with the basic Android platform, functioning in offline mode. We expect to improve this aspect by investigating speech recognition technologies specifically tailored to the medical context.

5 From Tracking to Assistance – Vision and Challenges

Besides tackling the trauma documentation problem, the Tracking Level is the base layer to devise on top different levels of assistance, which calls for designing more complex and interesting kind of PMDA agents. In this section we discuss the main ideas that we have about and that will be experimented in the Trauma Tracker Project.

5.1 From Monitoring and Warning Generation to Suggestions and Workflow

A first level of assistance is about the automatic generation of *warnings* that are displayed on the smart-glasses, about situations that the Trauma Leader may want to be notified without necessarily interrupting her activity flow. Situations may concern both the current state of the patient or its evolution – e.g., a warning could be generated if/when the value v of a vital parameter dynamically tracked by the system falls outside some predefined range $[min, max]$ –, and the temporal flow of actions carried on by the Trauma Team – e.g. some time t has elapsed after the administration of some drugs.

Situations can be modelled as predicates over the full context, including tracked information, current time and place where the Trauma Leader is, the identity trauma leader, and so on. This account for designing a PMDA which is capable of reasoning – at real-time – about the knowledge related to the temporal stream of data about the actions performed by the Trauma Team and about the evolution of the patient, and produce warnings. Such reasoning can be driven by rules defined by the Trauma Team. By exploiting the BDI model, such rules can be encoded into plans, reacting to relevant events and checking for the condition over beliefs encoding the context.

The kind of assistance discussed so far can be considered essentially *reactive*, i.e. the PMDA observes and reacts to events and situations occurring during the trauma management so as to notify warnings. A further kind of assistance which can be considered more *pro-active* accounts for a PMDA capable of reminding and suggesting the workflow of steps to follow in peculiar cases that require an ad-hoc treatment. In those cases, the trauma protocols and workflow to be adopted can be encoded in terms of goals and plans of the PMDA agent, yet preserving its reactive capabilities.

5.2 Integrating Cognitive Personal Assistant Agents with Cognitive Systems

In the model discussed so far, the generation of warnings and suggestions by the PMDA is based solely on the *local* knowledge about the ongoing trauma. A further step is to consider for that purpose also the *corpus* of knowledge related to trauma management and the documentation about the trauma done in the past, a big data collecting information from different hospital and trauma centers, and the use if *cognitive computing* techniques [13] to get insights from that Big Data. "cognitive computing" has been recently introduced by IBM [16] to refer to a set of tools and techniques – including Big Data and Analytics, machine learning, Internet of Things, Natural Language Processing, causal induction, probabilistic reasoning, and data visualization – which makes it possible to devise a "cognitive system" which is capable of learn, remember, analyse, resolve problems in specific contexts—healthcare and life science are a primary one [8]. The reference example developed by IBM of Cognitive System is Watson [16]. An interesting open research issue is then the design of PMDA that combines the capabilities of *cognitive agents* and the support of cloud-based *cognitive services* (Cognition-as-a-Service [39]) provided by cognitive systems such as Watson.

5.3 Towards Augmented Physicians Working in Augmented Hospitals

As already mentioned in the paper, wearable technologies promotes the design and use of hands-free or *on-the-go* interfaces [40, 41], that avoid as much as possible distracting the user from what she is doing – if not desired – and providing an information and suggestion flow which is seamlessly perceived and exploited by the user in her activity. This fosters a new perspective on the personal assistant running on this devices, like the PMDA.

Software Personal Agents explored in literature so far are based on the metaphor that of a *personal assistant* who is *collaborating with the user* in the same work environment [19]. The user interface of SPAs developed so far is mainly desktop or mobile, in which the SPA is often represented as a separate entity to interact with and to which the user delegates tasks. With wearable computing and handsfree interface, the SPA can be conceived more as *an extension of the self* [42], whose perceptions, beliefs, and possibly goals could be thought to be an extension of the user's ones, making the interaction more implicit and effective. Conceptually, the PMDA becomes an extension of the physician (*augmented physician*), augmenting her cognitive and practical capabilities.

This perspective goes toward the design of interface agents that – in spite of agent autonomy – should make the user always "feel in control" [11]. A main feature that could characterise this kind of personal agents would the capability to "see what the user sees" – by means of the camera on the eyewear device – and, more generally, to know what the user is perceiving about her context, given the sensors equipped with the device(s) worn by the user. This allows to frame a kind of pro-active assistance in which SPAs reason not only about the context of the user, but about what the user is perceiving – and not perceiving – from that context, what she is looking at, etc.

The definition and development of this kind of personal agents introduce interesting new research challenges for the agent community, partially tackled in related research context about eyewear computing [5], cognition-aware computing [4], activity-based computing [45] and context-aware computing [9]. These agents are meant to build dynamically a model about what the user is perceiving, and use this knowledge along with the information about user's goals, the state of ongoing activity, the actual state of the physical environment, to provide a pro-active and smart assistance, possibly anticipating and notifying problems and suggesting actions to do.

The full power of this idea can unleashed when the environment where the users are situated is *augmented* too, to provide functionalities and services that can be exploited by the Personal Medical Digital Assistant agents. Such augmentation can include two different levels, integrated:

- a software infrastructure layer running on computing devices embedded in hospital physical objects and environment;
- an augmented/mixed reality layer, composed by augmented entities enriching the physical reality, to be shared and perceived by the human users.

In literature, the first level is explored by research works on *pervasive health-care*, applying pervasive computing to the healthcare domain, including hospital environments [1]. In our case, this means the possibility for a PMDA agent to interact with hospital objects, devices and appliances turned into smart things in an Internet-of-Things (IoT) perspective, including output devices such wall displays. A further case which is relevant for the agent community is about adopting agents also for modeling and engineering the pervasive software layer, as investigated by research work in literature exploring agent-based ambient intelligence [12,32,33].

The second level concerns enriching the physical reality with *holograms* perceived by users by means of proper wearable devices (AR-enabled smart-glasses, visors), eventually shared among multiple users situated in the same augmented environment. Such virtual entities can range from simple information related to specific physical objects to virtual user interfaces and full-fledge animated virtual objects, eventually enriching the functionality of the physical environment. In our case, the Personal Medical Digital Assistant agent could be able to interact with holograms, eventually creating them according to the need.

The intertwining of these two augmentation levels leads to the idea of *augmented hospital* where (mobile) augmented reality technologies are integrated with pervasive ones so as to create novel kinds of smart environments [31], providing more advanced functionalities to support individual and cooperative work.

6   Conclusion and Future Work

Currently, the TraumaTracker prototype implements just the tracking functionality, which is however useful already to improve the quality of the trauma documentation and to automate the generation of trauma reports. Next steps will be devoted to develop and integrate higher functionality levels, along the vision depicted in Sect. 5. In particular, the very first next step will be to provide functionalities in terms of real-time assistance to the Trauma Leader/team, fully exploiting the hands-free characteristics of the system. The first kind of assistance which is being implemented is about the automatic generation of warnings that are displayed on the smart-glasses, about situations that the Trauma Leader may want to be notified without necessarily interrupting her activity flow. The modular design adopted for the Trauma Assistant Agent makes it possible to implement the extensions without substantially change the behaviour of the existing internal agents. For instance, we plan to implement the new assistance functionalities as a new Jason Monitoring Agent, which observes and reasons about the notes created in the Notes Stream artifact, generating proper warnings to be displayed through the Display Interface artifact.

Finally, our medium-term research objective accounts for *(i)* fully exploring the idea of an agent-based augmented hospital sketched in Sect. 5, starting from exploring the design of an augmented environment improving the work of healthcare professionals involved in trauma management, and *(ii)* devising proper models and architectures that allow to integrate cognitive agents – taking JaCaMo as reference technology – with cognitive computing systems, like Watson.

References

1. Bardram, J.E., Christensen, H.B.: Pervasive computing support for hospitals: an overview of the activity-based computing project. IEEE Pervasive Comput. **6**(1), 44–51 (2007)
2. Bardram, J., Baldus, H., Favela, J.: Pervasive computing in hospitals, pp. 48–77. CRC Press (2006)
3. Boissier, O., Bordini, R.H., Hübner, J.F., Ricci, A., Santi, A.: Multi-agent oriented programming with JaCaMo. Sci. Comput. Program. **78**(6), 747–761 (2013)
4. Bulling, A., Zander, T.O.: Cognition-aware computing. IEEE Pervasive Comput. **13**(3), 80–83 (2014)
5. Bulling, A., Cakmakci, O., Kunze, K., Rehg, J.M.: Eyewear Computing - Augmenting the Human with Head-mounted Wearable Assistants (Dagstuhl Seminar 16042). Dagstuhl Reports, vol. 6(1), pp. 160–206 (2016). http://drops.dagstuhl. de/opus/volltexte/2016/5820
6. Burstein, F., Zaslavsky, A., Arora, N.: Context-aware mobile agents for decision-making support in healthcare emergency applications. In: Workshop on Context Modeling and Decision Support (2005)
7. Chalupsky, H., Gil, Y., Knoblock, C.A., Lerman, K., Oh, J., Pynadath, D.V., Russ, T.A., Tambe, M.: Electric elves: Applying agent technology to support human organizations. In: Proceedings of the Thirteenth Conference on Innovative Applications of Artificial Intelligence Conference, pp. 51–58. AAAI Press (2001)
8. Chen, Y., Argentinis, J.E., Weber, G.: IBM Watson: How cognitive computing can be applied to big data challenges in life sciences research. Clin. Ther. **38**(4), 688–701 (2016)
9. Dey, A.K.: Understanding and using context. Personal Ubiquitous Comput. **5**(1), 4–7 (2001)
10. Domnori, E., Cabri, G., Leonardi, L.: Ubimedic2: an agent-based approach in territorial emergency management. In: 2011 5th International Conference on Pervasive Computing Technologies for Healthcare (PervasiveHealth) and Workshops, pp. 176–183, May 2011
11. Don, A., Brennan, S., Laurel, B., Shneiderman, B.: Anthropomorphism: from Eliza to terminator 2. In: Proceedings of the SIGCHI Conference on Human Factors in Computing Systems, CHI 1992, pp. 67–70. ACM, New York (1992)
12. Hagras, H., Callaghan, V., Colley, M., Clarke, G., Pounds-Cornish, A., Duman, H.: Creating an ambient-intelligence environment using embedded agents. IEEE Intell. Syst. **19**(6), 12–20 (2004)
13. Hurwitz, J., Kaufman, M., Bowles, A.: Cognitive Computing and Big Data Analytics. Wiley, Hoboken (2015)
14. Civil, I.D.S.: What is quality care in trauma? Injury **38**(5), 525–526 (2007)
15. Isern, D., Sánchez, D., Moreno, A.: Agents applied in health care: a review. Int. J. Med. Informatics **79**(3), 145–166 (2010)
16. Kelly, J.E.: Computing, cognition and the future of knowing. In: iBM Research and Solutions, white paper (2015)

17. Li, C., Giampapa, J.A., Sycara, K.P.: Bilateral negotiation decisions with uncertain dynamic outside options. IEEE Trans. Syst. Man Cybern. Part C **36**(1), 31–44 (2006)

18. Lindquist, M.A., Johansson, E.P., Petersson, I.G., Saveman, B.I., Nilsson, C.G.: The use of the personal digital assistant (PDA) among personnel and students in health care: a review. J. Med. Internet Res. **10**(4), e31 (2008)

19. Maes, P.: Agents that reduce work and information overload. Commun. ACM **37**(7), 30–40 (1994)

20. Mann, S.: Wearable computing as means for personal empowerment. In: Proceedings of the First International Conference on Wearable Computing(ICWC). IEEE Computer Society Press, Fairfax, VA, May 1998. http://www.eyetap.org/wearcam/icwc98/keynote.html

21. Mitchell, T.M., Caruana, R., Freitag, D., McDermott, J., Zabowski, D.: Experience with a learning personal assistant. Commun. ACM **37**(7), 80–91 (1994)

22. Modi, P.J., Veloso, M., Smith, S.F., Oh, J.: CMRadar: a personal assistant agent for calendar management. In: Bresciani, P., Giorgini, P., Henderson-Sellers, B., Low, G., Winikoff, M. (eds.) AOIS 2004. LNCS (LNAI), vol. 3508, pp. 169–181. Springer, Heidelberg (2005). https://doi.org/10.1007/11426714_12

23. Newman, S., Steed, L., Mulligan, K.: Self-management interventions for chronic illness. Lancet **364**(9444), 1523–1537 (2004)

24. O'Connor, T., Raposo, E.A., Heller-Wescott, T.: Improving trauma documentation in the emergency department. J. Trauma Nurs. **21**(5), 238–243 (2014)

25. Okamoto, S., Scerri, P., Sycara, K.: Toward an understanding of the impact of software personal assistants on human organizations. In: Proceedings of the Fifth International Joint Conference on Autonomous Agents and Multiagent Systems, AAMAS 2006, pp. 630–637. ACM, New York (2006)

26. Omicini, A., Ricci, A., Viroli, M.: Artifacts in the A&A meta-model for multi-agent systems. Auton. Agent. Multi-Agent Syst. **17**(3), 432–456 (2008)

27. Orwat, C., Graefe, A., Faulwasser, T.: Towards pervasive computing in health care - a literature review. BMC Med. Inform. Decis. Mak. **8**(1), 26 (2008)

28. Poggi, A., Bergenti, F.: Developing smart emergency applications with multi-agent systems. Int. J. e-Health Med. Commun. **1**(4), 1–13 (2010)

29. Rao, A.S.: AgentSpeak(L): BDI agents speak out in a logical computable language. In: Van de Velde, W., Perram, J.W. (eds.) MAAMAW 1996. LNCS, vol. 1038, pp. 42–55. Springer, Heidelberg (1996). https://doi.org/10.1007/BFb0031845

30. Rao, A.S., Georgeff, M.P.: BDI agents: from theory to practice. In: Lesser, V.R., Gasser, L. (eds.) 1st International Conference on Multi Agent Systems (ICMAS 1995), pp. 312–319. The MIT Press, San Francisco, CA, USA, 12–14 June 1995

31. Ricci, A., Piunti, M., Tummolini, L., Castelfranchi, C.: The mirror world: preparing for mixed-reality living. IEEE Pervasive Comput. **14**(2), 60–63 (2015)

32. Rodríguez, M.D., Favela, J., Preciado, A., Vizcaíno, A.: Agent-based ambient intelligence for healthcare. AI Commun. **18**(3), 201–216 (2005)

33. Sadri, F.: Ambient intelligence: a survey. ACM Comput. Surv. **43**(4), 36:1–36:66 (2011)

34. Santi, A., Guidi, M., Ricci, A.: JaCa-Android: an agent-based platform for building smart mobile applications. In: Dastani, M., Fallah Seghrouchni, A., Hübner, J., Leite, J. (eds.) LADS 2010. LNCS (LNAI), vol. 6822, pp. 95–114. Springer, Heidelberg (2011). https://doi.org/10.1007/978-3-642-22723-3_6

35. Sarcevic, A.: "Who's scribing?": documenting patient encounter during trauma resuscitation. In: Proceedings of the SIGCHI Conference on Human Factors in Computing Systems, CHI 2010, pp. 1899–1908. ACM, New York (2010)

36. Shankararaman, V., Ambrosiadou, V., Loomes, M., Panchal, T.: Patient care management using a multi-agent approach. In: 2000 IEEE International Conference on Systems, Man, and Cybernetics, vol. 3, pp. 1817–1821 (2000)
37. Shintani, T., Ito, T., Sycara, K.: Multiple negotiations among agents for a distributed meeting scheduler. In: Proceedings of the Fourth International Conference on Multi Agent Systems (ICMAS-2000), p. 435. IEEE Computer Society, Washington, DC, USA (2000)
38. Silva, B.M., Rodrigues, J.J., de la Torre Díez, I., López-Coronado, M., Saleem, K.: Mobile-health: a review of current state in 2015. J. Biomed. Inform. **56**, 265–272 (2015)
39. Spohrer, J., Banavar, G.: Cognition as a service: an industry perspective. AI Mag. **36**(4), 71–86 (2015)
40. Starner, T.: The challenges of wearable computing: part 1. IEEE Micro **21**(4), 44–52 (2001)
41. Starner, T.: The challenges of wearable computing: part 2. IEEE Micro **21**(4), 54–67 (2001)
42. Starner, T.: Project glass: an extension of the self. IEEE Pervasive Comput. **12**(2), 14–16 (2013)
43. Starner, T., Mann, S., Rhodes, B., Levine, J., Healey, J., Kirsch, D., Picard, R.W., Pentland, A.: Augmented reality through wearable computing. Presence Teleoper. Virtual Environ. **6**(4), 386–398 (1998)
44. Su, C.J., Wu, C.Y.: JADE implemented mobile multi-agent based, distributed information platform for pervasive health care monitoring. Appl. Soft Comput. **11**(1), 315–325 (2011)
45. Sukthankar, R., Davies, N., Siewiorek, D.P.: Activity-based computing. IEEE Pervasive Comput. **7**, 20–21 (2008)
46. Taboada, M., Cabrera, E., Iglesias, M.L., Epelde, F., Luque, E.: An agent-based decision support system for hospitals emergency departments. Procedia Comput. Sci. **4**, 1870–1879 (2011)
47. Tambe, M.: Electric Elves: what went wrong and why. AI Mag. **29**(2), 23–27 (2008)
48. Tentori, M., Hayes, G.R., Reddy, M.: Pervasive computing for hospital, chronic, and preventive care. Found. Trends®Hum.-Comput. Interact. **5**(1), 1–95 (2012)
49. de la Torre, A.B., Lluch-Ariet, M., Pegueroles-Vallés, J.: Security analysis of a protocol based on multi agents systems for clinical data exchange. In: 2013 Seventh International Conference on Complex, Intelligent, and Software Intensive Systems, pp. 305–311, July 2013
50. Varshney, U.: Mobile health: four emerging themes of research. Decis. Support Syst. **66**, 20–35 (2014)
51. Wagner, T., Phelps, J., Guralnik, V., VanRiper, R.: Coordinators: coordination managers for first responders. In: Proceedings of the Third International Joint Conference on Autonomous Agents and Multi agent Systems, AAMAS 2004, vol. 3, pp. 1140–1147. IEEE Computer Society, Washington, DC, USA (2004)
52. Whitten, P., Holtz, B., LaPlante, C.: Telemedicine: what have we learned? Appl. Clin. Inform. **1**(2), 132–141 (2010)

A System for the Management of Clinical Tasks Throughout the Clinical Process with Notification Features

António Silva[1] , Tiago Oliveira[2](✉) , José Neves[1] , Ken Satoh[2], and Paulo Novais[1]

[1] Algoritmi Centre/Department of Informatics, University of Minho, Braga, Portugal
asilva@algoritmi.uminho.pt, {jneves,pjon}@di.uminho.pt
[2] National Institute of Informatics, Tokyo, Japan
{toliveira,ksatoh}@nii.ac.jp

Abstract. Computer-Interpretable Guidelines have been associated with a higher integration of standard practices in the daily context of health care institutions. The Clinical Decision Support Systems that deliver these machine-interpretable recommendations usually follow a Q&A style of communication, retrieving information from the user or a clinical repository and performing reasoning upon it, based on the rules from Clinical Practice Guidelines. However, these systems are limited in the reach they are capable of achieving as they were initially conceived for use in very specific moments of the clinical process, namely in physician appointments. The purpose of this work is thus to present a system that, in addition to Q&A reasoning, is equipped with other functionalities such as the scheduling and temporal management of clinical tasks, the mapping of these tasks onto an agenda of activities to allow an easy consultation by health care professionals, and notifications that let health care professionals know of task enactment times and information collection times. In this way, the system ensures the delivery of procedures. The main components of the system, which reflect a different perspective on the delivery of CIG advice that we call guideline as a service, are disclosed, and they include a health care Personal Assistant Web Application, a health care assistant mobile application, and the integration with the private calendar services of the user.

1 Introduction

Computer-Interpretable Guidelines (CIGs) are machine-interpretable versions of Clinical Practice Guidelines (CPGs). The latter are systematically developed statements associated with the promotion of best medical practices and reduction of medical error [21]. The aim of these documents is to provide clinical advice for specific circumstances and to support health care professionals in their decisions [10]. Their formalisation as CIGs in Clinical Decision Support Systems (CDSSs) brings forth the development of a new range of operations that can be

S. Montagna et al. (Eds.): A2HC 2017/A-HEALTH 2017, LNAI 10685, pp. 76–93, 2017.
https://doi.org/10.1007/978-3-319-70887-4_5

performed with the knowledge they enclose. Such include automated reasoning for the generation of recommendations, consistency checking within the same CIG and across different CIGs, and merging CIG knowledge with contextual information such as patient and physician preferences or available health care resources, to name a few [16]. The point of these operations is to tailor care in order to generate better outcomes and avoid adverse events. Nonetheless, managing patients is a challenging endeavour for health care professionals given that they are typically responsible for numerous cases at the same time and each case involves the enactment of several and complex procedures. Managing this complexity is something that the current applications for CIG execution do not contemplate in the functionalities they offer [2, 23–25]. Current CIG-based systems do not provide mechanisms for integrating CIG recommendations in the daily routine of health care institutions, which calls forth the need for such systems to assume a new style of communication that can further promote a positive impact on the outcomes of care [11].

CIGs are considered to be the best approach to the concept of *living guidelines*, which captures statements for clinical decision support that are dynamic - in the sense that they are capable of evolving and providing advice based on the latest evidence - and interactive [8]. This interactive component is related to the ability to cover tasks such as patient tracking, patient follow-up, scheduling of procedures, and the monitoring of procedure constraints, and, at the same time, autonomously inform health care professionals about important aspects of these procedures in the most diverse situations.

Following the identified need for different ways in which to deliver CIG-based advice, the work herein proposes a different perspective regarding this matter. Its main contribution is a system that allows different implementations of CIGs. We show how these implementations can be differently oriented through a Personal Assistant Web Application and a health care assistant mobile app. The principle behind the system and the presented implementations is that the constraints supported my a CIG model and placed on clinical tasks can be used to enhance CIG-based CDSSs. The system is based on the CompGuide ontology for CIGs [14], which treats CPGs as sets of various clinical tasks organised in a work flow. The present paper represents an extension of the work in [22].

Section 2 describes related work regarding systems for CIG execution, featuring a description of their means of operation. In Sect. 3, we present the CompGuide ontology and respective main features that led to the implementations described in the following section. Section 4 provides details about the CompGuide architecture for the deployment of CIGs and how its services are used as a basis for the Personal Assistant Web Application and the health care assistant mobile application developed to accompany health care professionals. Section 5 describes the functionalities supporting care with examples of CIG execution. Finally, Sect. 6 presents the conclusions drawn so far with the development of the health care assistant and future directions for the work.

2   Existing Systems for CIG Execution

Based on the classification of CDSSs presented in [11] - tools for information management, tools for patient-specific advice, and tools for focusing attention - and the analysis of current CIG execution approaches [6], it is possible to observe that the most significant examples fall under the category of tools for patient-specific advice. This is the case of CIG execution engines such as the GLIF3, Guideline Execution Engine (GLEE) [24], the Spock Engine [25], and the GLARE Execution Engine [23], which were specifically developed for the application of guidelines to patients in health care settings.

GLEE [24] is based on the third version of the Guideline Interchange Format (GLIF3) [3], which, in turn, was designed to support guideline modelling as a flowchart of structured steps that represented clinical actions and decisions. The architecture of GLEE provides three layers of *abstraction*, namely *data, business logic* and *user interface*. The *data* layer contains an electronic medical record with patient data, a guideline repository, and a clinical event monitor that allows the execution of CIGs driven by clinical events. The *business logic* layer contains an execution engine consisting of a server and many clients that interact with users. The bottom interface layer contains the applications responsible for exchanging information with the upper layers. The execution engine records every clinical parameter from a patient during the execution of a CIG, suggesting actions to be performed. In addition, the user can control the process by confirming or deciding different transitions between actions.

The Spock Engine [25] was developed to enable the execution of CIGs in the Asbru model [19]. It incorporates an inference engine that can retrieve data from the patient's electronic medical record. It is a modular client-server application that consists of a set of classes to store guidelines, a parser to interpret their content and a synchronizer that establishes the communication with external systems. This execution engine stores different data structures such as state transitions, a queue of scheduled awaiting tasks, and the list of recommendations already issued. This strict control of tasks stems from the expressiveness of the Asbru temporal model, which provides various temporal patterns for the control of recommendation steps.

The GLARE Execution Engine was also developed based on a CIG model focused on temporal constraints, the Guideline Acquisition, Representation and Execution (GLARE) [23]. CIGs in GLARE follow a proprietary graph-based structure, where a clinical action is represented by a node. It is possible to define atomic actions like queries to obtain information, work actions that represent medical procedures, decision actions with sets of conditions, and conclusions that describe the output of a decision. Similarly to the other systems, GLARE also defines three abstraction layers. In this case they are called *system, xml,* and *dbms.* The system layer contains an execution interface tied to an execution engine that interprets and updates XML files representing instances of patients and guideline executions in the *xml* layer. These are intermediate structures used to exchange data with the *dbms* layer and the *system* layer in a structured way.

All these systems use structures and well-defined languages that can be read and analysed by a program. Furthermore, they also feature a guideline repository, a run-time engine for the CIG knowledge, and an electronic medical record. Furthermore, they may, as in the case of the GLARE Execution Engine, support modules that describe the context, mainly in terms of available resources, of the health care institution where CIG deployment is taking place. Their objective is to run CIG instructions against data from patients and produce tailored recommendations, according to the observed state. In these systems, the role of the execution engine is straightforward, in the sense that it is merely concerned with following the constraints of the clinical work flow, comparing items of the patient state with conditions stated in rules dictating whether a recommendation should be provided or not. Most applications for CIG execution, including the above-given examples, exist in the form of client-server applications, with the intelligence engine placed on the client side. Furthermore, these applications are mostly available as desktop applications, which is an obstacle to their potential for reaching health care professionals and their ease of deployment.

The idea of enhancing CDSSs with additional features that allow them to achieve a higher level of integration of clinical recommendations in clinical practice comes from the ever-increasing role of Ambient Assisted Living (AAL) in enabling new information and communication services which transparently support people in their everyday lives [9, 12]. In fact, a similar idea has been explored in [4], where a personal memory assistant, capable of intelligent scheduling and deployed over a platform, called iGenda. The assistant acts as the support for a centralised manager system that can manage several services and is responsible for the scheduling of multiple agendas, taking into account the availability of resources or the health conditions of the users. Although different, the work proposed herein can be related to this project and others such as the Collaborative Memory Aids [17] and Hermes [7], but with the focus placed on the health care professional.

3   CompGuide Ontology for Clinical Practice Guidelines

The CIG model used in this work is the CompGuide ontology [14]. It provides representation primitives for clinical recommendations based on Web Ontology Language (OWL) by following a task network model in which each recommendation assumes the form of a task. In order to reflect this, a set of key OWL classes were defined as subclasses of *ClinicalTask*. They include the folllowing:

- *Action*: a task that should be performed by a health care professional such as an observation, procedure, exam, or treatment application;
- *Question*: a task to get information about the clinical parameters that build the state of the patient;
- *Decision*: a task that encodes a decision regarding the state of a patient, featuring various options and respective conditions;
- *Plan*: a composed task containing instances of the other tasks defined to achieve a specific goal.

In CompGuide there are object properties that connect instances of the classes as mentioned above in order to define the relative order between tasks. In this regard, it is possible to define: sequential tasks, parallel tasks which should be executed simultaneously, and alternative tasks from which one is automatically selected for execution. In this sense, a guideline in CompGuide resembles a linked list of recommendations.

Additionally, it is possible to define different types of conditions that constrain task execution, including trigger conditions to select one amongst alternative tasks, pre-conditions which must be verified before executing a task, conditions for options in *Decision* tasks, and expected outcomes for clinical tasks. The *Condition* class allows the representation of these conditions with specific properties for clinical parameters and their values.

The classes that enable the representation of temporal restrictions are all subclasses of *TemporalElement* [15]. The relationship between these temporal classes and the classes in ClinicalTask are shown in Fig. 1, along with the properties used to connect them. One of the subclasses of *TemporalElement* is *TemporalUnit* which represents the different units in which a temporal constraint may be expressed. It is an enumerated class consisting of the instances *second*, *minute*, *hour*, *day*, *week*, *month*, and *year*. The main classes that enable the definition of temporal restrictions about the execution of tasks are:

- *Duration*: definition of how long *Actions* and *Plans* should last.
- *WaitingTime*: definition of a delay in the start of a clinical task.
- *Periodicity*: definition of the frequency of a clinical task.
- *CyclePartPeriodicity*: a nested temporal pattern for the definition of a periodicity within a periodicity.

Temporal reasoning about the state of a patient is enabled by the *TemporalRestriction* class, whose instances can be associated with a *Condition* through the *hasTemporalRestriction* property. With the *hasTemporalOperator* property a *TemporalOperator* is specified for the restriction. *TemporalOperator* consists of two instances, *within_the_last* and *within_the_following*. The operator *within_the_last* is used when one aims to express that a condition about the patient state must have held true at least once, within a period of time just before execution time. It is used in trigger conditions, pre-conditions and conditions of rules in *Decision* instances. This operator is interpreted by checking if, in the state of the patient, there is a record regarding the parameter in the condition, registered within the specified time frame, whose value validates the condition. As for the *within_the_following* operator, it expresses a condition about the future, in which one aims to observe the effect a clinical task has after being applied to a patient. Such conditions are used in task outcomes. Within the context of a CPG for the diagnosis and treatment of colon cancer, an example of a temporal restriction would be an *Action* that advised chemotherapy with an outcome stating that the tumour should become operable within six months. In this case, there is a condition with a temporal restriction featuring a *within_the_following* operator.

The details of the CompGuide model are further provided in [15], along with an assessment of the expressiveness of the model compared to other approaches

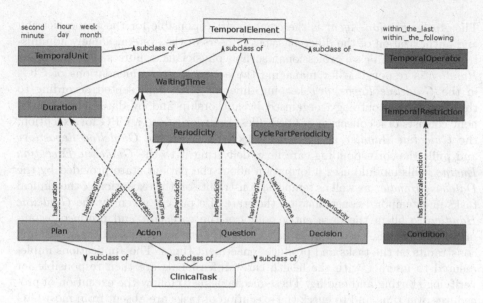

Fig. 1. Representation of the CompGuide ontology with clinical tasks and respective temporal elements.

that revealed that it enables the representation of more temporal patterns. The interpretation of the work flow of tasks, their clinical constraints, and their temporal constraints demands an execution engine capable of analysing these three aspects and crossing them with patient information. However, these instructions may become too intricate for a clear understanding, which demands ways of delivering CIGs that also help to manage the complexity of these recommendations during their enactment.

4   CompGuide Architecture for CIG Execution

The CompGuide system follows a service-oriented architecture that aims to provide recommendations to support medical decision-making. As shown in Fig. 2, it consists of a *Core Server* that is the central component of the architecture and was developed as a RESTful web service application. The usage of web services as the means to access the *Core Server* offers consistent performance to access the web resources, better scalability and modifiability, providing the possibility of improving selected services without compromising others. This architectural style grants greater flexibility when integrating CIG execution functionalities in third party applications [13]. Given the architecture style used for the system and the concept of a centralised CIG management system that allows different implementations, the distribution of CompGuide follows a *software as a service* (Saas) model.

The *Core Server* has four modules: the *Authentication Agent*, the *Guideline Handler*, the *Database Handler* and the *Guideline Execution Engine*.

The *Authentication Agent* is the component responsible for the authentication and authorization of the different types of users of the system, namely administrators and health care professional, such as physicians or nurses. The *Guideline Handler* is responsible for managing the access to recommendations of CIGs in the *Guideline Repository*, keeping different CIGs represented according to the CompGuide ontology, organised by authorship and by date. This component consists of a collection of OWL files. In order to use a CPG for execution, the *Guideline Handler* accesses the selected CIG in the *Guideline Repository* and pulls the corresponding care flow, delivering it to the *Guideline Execution Engine*. This module uses information about the patient state provided by the *Database Handler* as well as temporal constraints on the execution of the clinical tasks and temporal constraints on the state of a patient given by the *Guideline Handler* to fill in the data entry points of the care flow and produce recommendations. Thus, the *Guideline Execution Engine* interprets all the scheduling constraints on the tasks and produces enactment times. The applications implemented to interact with the health care professionals are then responsible for verifying starting and ending. These mechanisms to follow the execution of procedures over time and to check the execution of tasks are absent from most CIG frameworks [20], but they are essential to have a decision support that is truly capable of following up on guideline deployment.

The *Core Server*, as mentioned before, provides these features as RESTful web services implemented in Java, using the RESTEasy API over a WildFly Application Server. The Personal Assistant Web Application, which uses the web services available in the *Core Server*, was developed as a web application following the Model-View-Control (MVC) paradigm using Java Server Faces (JSF). The *Health Care Assistant Mobile App*lication is an android application developed in Java, which also uses the same web services. The purpose of the *Core Server* is to make available CIG services that anyone can integrate into their own applications, with a special focus on AAL applications. Following the parallel with Saas, this form of delivering CIGs can be considered to be *guideline as a service*.

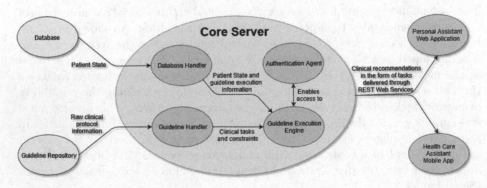

Fig. 2. Architecture of CompGuide system

4.1   CompGuide RESTful Web Services

The CompGuide web services provide a set of features that allows accessing the *Guideline Repository* as well as saving, removing and updating information in the *Database*. Their description is as follows.

The *Guideline Service* handles the logic of the execution of a guideline, task to task, obtaining codified tasks in the ontology, providing them as recommendations. The *Get Tasks Service* provides a list of tasks that must be executed at a given moment. In order to get the next task to be executed, the user must perform a request to the *Next Task Service*.

The *Guidelines Service* has only one web service that provides the list of existing guidelines in the data base. Additionally, the *Guideline Execution Service* represents the execution of a guideline initiated by a physician and associated with a patient, so this web service provides information about the execution of a guideline. To add a new execution, the user must perform a request to the *Add Guideline Execution Service*. Regarding the *Guideline Execution Active Service*, this web service provides a list of the active executions of guidelines for a specific user.

It is also possible to retrieve and alter patient information through the *Patient Service*, which allows to add, remove, update and retrieve patient information.

Finally, the *Task Service* and *User Service* follow the same structure of the previous services, allowing the access and manipulation of information about these respective entities in the *Database*.

4.2   Personal Assistant Web Application

The *Personal Assistant Web Application* is an application that highlights the role of CPGs as patient management and following tools. Based on the information provided by the *Execution Engine*, it can keep track of clinical tasks that should be carried out by the health care professional. By using information and communication systems, it is possible to provide CIGs with dynamism, presence, and interactivity that may bring them closer to the concept of living guidelines. It enables the management of information about CPGs, health care professionals that are users in the system, and patients to which CPGs are applied. As such, one can create, edit and delete all this information, according to the type of authorization in the system.

In order to facilitate the visualisation of the clinical tasks, for the health care professionals, the application provides two forms of displaying these recommendations. The first is a timeline in which all the clinical tasks are shown over a chronogram. A timeline of activities has the ability to compress multiple tasks into a single continuity without compromising the succession, and the easy understanding of clinical procedures. The benefits from such a representation include the capacity to sequence events and reduce the potential for overburdening the health care professional. Additionally, by visualising all of the pieces of a guideline treatment, care providers can make more focused, effective decisions about resources and timetables. This view is shown in Fig. 3. In it, it is possible to observe clinical tasks for the management of colon cancer, namely sequential workup actions to ascertain the state of the patient.

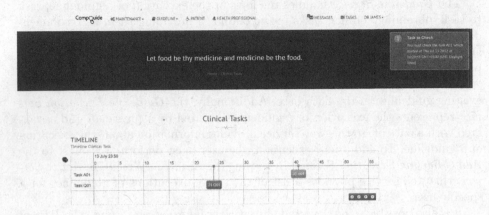

Fig. 3. Timeline view of clinical procedures in the CompGuide Personal Assistant Web Application.

The other available view is a calendar in which the health care professional can visualise the tasks according to the temporal granularity he sees fit, namely week, day, and month. While with the timeline it is easier to detect the starting and ending points of tasks, with the calendar view it is easier to grasp the temporal constraints that bind clinical tasks such as durations, waiting times and periodicities. Figure 4 shows the same tasks as in the timeline, but displayed over a week, where it is possible to verify, for instance, for how long a clinical task should be applied. The purpose of the calendar view is to avoid overlooking tasks and dismissing them as that may have an adverse impact on the evolution of the patient.

In order to ensure the execution of tasks at the designated time, it was necessary to implement a notification system and a message box. These elements are both shown in Fig. 5. The message box features messages such as indications about the tasks that should be performed or should have already been performed, offering the possibility to mark them as executed. As for the notification system, it is used to periodically alert the user about task enactment times and steps to collect information about the patient, such as the outcomes of clinical tasks, according to their respective temporal restrictions. The notifications are shown as a pop-up message.

Fig. 4. Calendar view of clinical procedures in the CompGuide Personal Assistant Web Application.

4.3   Health Care Assistant Mobile Application

In order to improve patient monitoring to increase the efficiency when treating the patients and the preparation for the appointments by the health care professionals, we developed a mobile solution. The mobile application allows the physicians or nurses to consult and monitor the progress of patients as well as the clinical recommendations wherever they need to.

The application uses the CompGuide web services to request all the patient data and clinical tasks, whereby the recommendations are displayed in a calendar of clinical procedures that was implemented using the Custom Calendar library [18]. The clinical tasks are the same that can be seen in the web application, since these two assistants, the web and mobile application, use the centralised RESTful web service developed in the *Core Server*. The fact that all the data is centralised in only one component allows a better tracking of the user actions, greater control over his decisions and get constant supply of clinical recommendations.

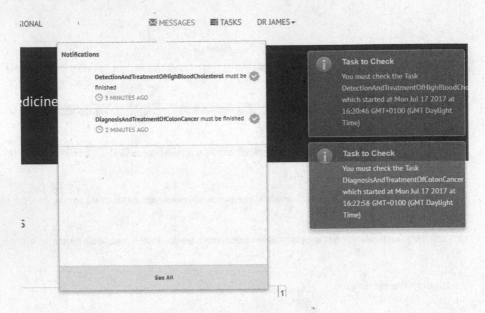

Fig. 5. Message box and notification in the CompGuide Personal Assistant Web Application.

Fig. 6. Calendar view of clinical procedures in the mobile application.

The calendar widget provides the view and methods necessary to display a calendar and schedule events. With this calendar, it is possible to navigate through the months and by clicking on a particular date, all the events for that day are shown below in the calendar, as depicted in Fig. 6.

Its main objectives are to provide timely clinical recommendations and integrate them in the clinical practice of the health care professional. As future work, a push notification feature can be implemented in order to inform the users of when they should execute clinical tasks, when they should start them and when they should finish them.

4.4   Integration with Google Calendar

The Google calendar API was developed to allow the integration of applications with Google calendar and its features. The managing of events and the push notifications are the most interesting features, the user can use to monitor and supervise the clinical tasks to take control of all patient parameters and clinical process. With this API, it is possible to manage the information regarding the clinical recommendations as well as oversee and follow-up these tasks anytime and anywhere with only a mobile device. Thus, both health care assistants can sync the calendar present in CompGuide with their Google calendar account. The Google calendar provides a public RESTful API that allows the integration with a variety of devices and services on the internet. This API lets the users display, create and modify calendar events as well as work with many other calendar-related objects, such as calendars or access controls [5]. Furthermore, its Java API is native to the Android operating system, allowing a possible integration in the future with the mobile application.

Regarding the integration of the API, firstly it was necessary the registration of the application in the Google console, and then the download of Google credentials, to use in the application. After these credentials were integrated into the project, it was possible to communicate with the API. This REST API can be utilised by making explicit HTTP calls, but there are client libraries implemented in various programming languages that make the API easier to use. Thus, we used the Java client library, since the web and mobile assistants are implemented in Java.

To export the clinical tasks, presented in the calendar view of the CompGuide web assistant, it is necessary to click on the "Export to Google Calendar" button. This view is shown in Fig. 4(a). After this action, the user will be redirected to the Google consent screen, asking to authorise the CompGuide application to request some user data. If the user approves, then Google gives a temporary access token that allows the application to request user data. Therefore, the CompGuide will attach the access token to the request, process all the clinical tasks and its temporal constraints, in order to create the events into the Google calendar of the user.

Through the Google calendar application, the users can see the clinical tasks and their details by clicking on the task, as shown in Fig. 7(b).

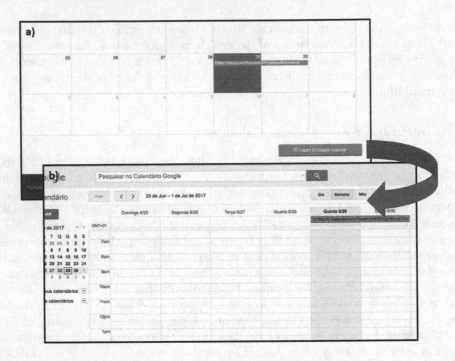

Fig. 7. Calendar view of clinical procedures in Google calendar.

5 Execution Examples

To test our temporal ontology, we used the NCCN Clinical Practice Guideline for Colon Cancer [1]. Its representation resulted in an OWL file containing 223 task instances, of which: 190 were Action tasks, 21 were Question tasks, one was a Decision task, and 11 were Plans. Out of the 223 tasks, a total of 95 had temporal constraints. The representation of the NCCN guideline in the model was carried out using Protégé, an ontology editor for OWL. 4.1. This CPG includes procedures that unfold over different phases of treatment, from cancer staging to follow-up, and presents a wide variety of temporal patterns. The most abundant pattern was the *Periodicity*, mainly because of the rich description of chemotherapy regimens made in this protocol.

As demonstrated in [15], the temporal ontology was able to represent effectively all the temporal patterns in the CPG, with a special focus on *Durations* and *Periodicites*, since they were the most frequent temporal aspects. Considering an example of a task in the form of a clinical *Action* from the CPG, which we will refer to as Example 1 from now on, the use of a *Duration* constructor may be derived from the following description "perform neoadjuvant therapy for six months". In it, the *Action* consists in neoadjuvant therapy (a term used to refer to chemotherapy or radiotherapy) before treatment with a *Duration* expressed using an exact duration value of six and a temporal unit of month.

Regarding periodic tasks, most of them were also bounded by a *Duration*. The constraints followed a structure similar to the one in the recommendation "apply medication for neoadjuvant therapy every two weeks for two-three months", which we will consider as Example 2. It is possible to identify the *Action* to apply medication for neoadjuvant therapy, the periodicity value of two with a temporal unit of week, a minimum duration value of two, a maximum duration value of three, and the respective temporal unit of month. In this case, the execution engine would recommend the execution of the task with the specified frequency at least for two months and at most for three.

The *Guideline Execution Engine* from the CompGuide architecture is used to produce inferences that ultimately result in recommendations of clinical tasks. Once these recommendations are retrieved, their constraints (in this case, their temporal constraints) are interpreted by the Personal Assistant Web Application and mapped onto the different views mentioned earlier. With this, for Example 1, an event with a duration of 6 months is created, starting on the 18th of July of 2017, as shown in Fig. 8(a), and finishing on the 16th of January of 2018, as can be seen in Fig. 8(c). The corresponding result for the expression that concerns Example 2 consists of a set of events that repeat every two weeks, so the application will unfold the recommendation in multiple events and register them in the timeline. Although the execution engine would recommend the execution of the task with the frequency at least for two months and at most for three, the *Personal Assistant Web Application* will display the maximum duration

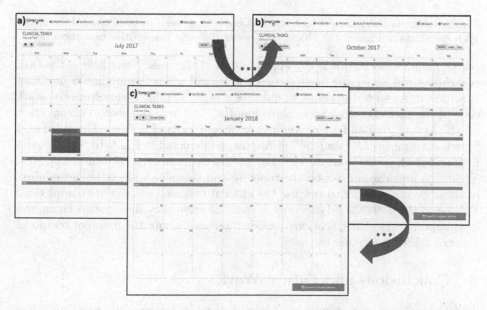

Fig. 8. Execution of a clinical task from Example 1, as can be seen in the Personal Assistant Web Application. Figures (a), (b), and (c) show different consecutive execution times.

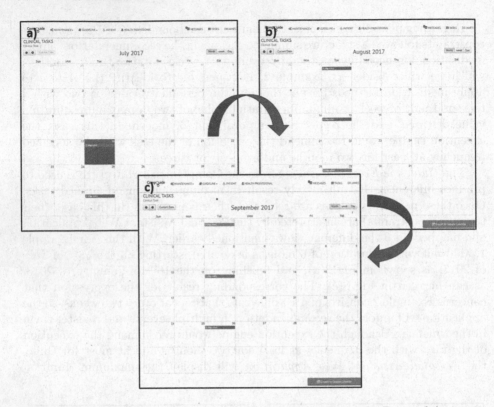

Fig. 9. Execution of a clinical task from Example 2, as seen in the Personal Assistant Web Application. Figures (a), (b), and (c) show different consecutive execution times.

(three months) because it is the upper bound of the task. Nonetheless, the task controllers will notify the health care professional when the minimum duration is achieved. As such, the result would be six new calendar events from the start date of the task execution up to three months. The first and second events start on the 18th of July and 1st of August, as shown in the Fig. 9(a). The third and fourth start on the 15th and 29th of August, as depicted in Fig. 9(b). Finally, the fifth and sixth events start on 12th and 26th of September, as shown in Fig. 9(c). Then, the user can consult on the timeline and calendar widgets the scheduling of these events in order to execute the clinical task and manage its completion. Whenever the users should execute the tasks or when they should start them, the application provides notifications, as side messages, about the different temporal constraints, thus alerting the user.

6   Conclusions and Future Work

The CompGuide system presented herein aims to increase the reach of CIGs beyond the medical office. The purpose of the different implementations is to ensure the timely enactment of clinical procedures over the course of patient management, removing the possibility of inadvertently skipping steps that may prove to be crucial later on for his recovery. In addition to decision support functionalities, common to other CIG systems, the CompGuide system allows the development of additional scheduling and alert features to assist the health care professional in keeping track of their patients. Therefore, its main contribution is a new method to integrate CPG advice in a clinical setting and make it easily available. The *Guideline Execution Engine* included in the *Core Server* establishes the relative order of tasks to be executed and their execution times based on the clinical information retrieved from the patient. This is the most complex part of CIG deployment, given the complexity, the procedural and temporal patterns of CPGs may show. Once these constraints are produced and delivered through a distribution model, in the form of guideline as a service, it becomes possible to develop reminder tools like the ones described herein. Here lies a development that can close the gap between CPGs and practitioners and promote the integration of evidence-based clinical advice in AAL monitoring systems.

This mapping of the clinical tasks onto a temporal execution line raises a relevant question. The *modus operandi* of the Personal Assistant Web Application is to issue notifications and alerts in order to promote compliance from the physician. However, if tasks are not executed at their appropriate times, the tool only issues alerts and allows the physician to skip the task and move to the next one. There are other methods to manage this situation, but all of them have drawbacks. Re-scheduling the task may imply verifying if the state of the patient allows the enactment of the procedure at a later time. Not performing the task may be equally damaging to the patient. Such an issue will be under consideration in future developments of the system. Additionally, we recognise the need for an evaluation of the system and both the Personal Assistant Web Application and the health care assistant mobile app. Such can be done by through an experiment in which a physician uses the system and its two implementations to obtain advice about the patients he is responsible for. In addition to usability assessments, with this experiment, it will be possible to compare the recommendations provided by the system to those the health care professional would usually issue. It is our intention to conduct this study and obtain an assessment of the fitness of the system to CIG deployment.

Acknowledgements. This work has been supported by COMPETE: POCI-01-0145-FEDER-0070 43 and FCT – Fundação para a Ciência e Tecnologia within the Project Scope UID/CEC/ 00319/2013.

References

1. Benson, A., Bekaii-Saab, T., Chan, E., Chen, Y.J., Choti, M., Cobper, H., Engstrom, P.: NCCN clinical practice guideline in oncology colon cancer. Technical report, National Comprehensive Cancer Network (2013)
2. Berg, D., Ram, P., Glasgow, J., Castro, J.: SAGEDesktop: an environment for testing clinical practice guidelines. In: The 26th Annual International Conference of the IEEE Engineering in Medicine and Biology Society, vol. 4, pp. 3217–3220 (2004)

3. Boxwala, A.A., Peleg, M., Tu, S., Ogunyemi, O., Zeng, Q.T., Wang, D., Patel, V.L., Greenes, R.A., Shortliffe, E.H.: GLIF3: a representation format for sharable computer-interpretable clinical practice guidelines. J. Biomed. Inform. **37**(3), 147–161 (2004)

4. Costa, A., Novais, P., Corchado, J.M., Neves, J.: Increased performance and better patient attendance in an hospital with the use of smart agendas*. Logic J. IGPL **20**(4), 689 (2012)

5. Google Developers: Get Started with the Calendar API (2016). https://developers.google.com/google-apps/calendar/overview

6. Isern, D., Moreno, A.: Computer-based execution of clinical guidelines: a review. Int. J. Med. Inform. **77**(12), 787–808 (2008)

7. Jiang, J., Khelifi, F., Trundle, P., Geven, A.: HERMES: a FP7 funded project towards the development of a computer-aided memory management system via intelligent computations. J. Assistive Technol. **3**(3), 27–35 (2009)

8. Kaiser, K., Miksch, S.: Versioning computer-interpretable guidelines: semi-automatic modeling of 'Living Guidelines' using an information extraction method. Artif. Intell. Med. **46**(1), 55–66 (2009)

9. Lima, L., Novais, P., Neves, J., Bulas, C.J., Costa, R.: Group decision making and quality-of-information in e-health systems. Logic J. IGPL **19**(2), 315–332 (2011)

10. Lohr, K.N., Field, M.J., et al.: Clinical Practice Guidelines: Directions for a New Program, vol. 90. National Academies Press, Washington, DC (1990)

11. Musen, M.A., Shahar, Y., Shortliffe, E.H.: Clinical decision-support systems. In: Shortliffe, E., Cimino, J. (eds.) Biomedical Informatics. Health Informatics, pp. 698–736. Springer, New York (2006). https://doi.org/10.1007/978-0-387-21721-5_16

12. Novais, P., Costa, R., Carneiro, D., Neves, J.: Inter-organization cooperation for ambient assisted living. J. Ambient Intell. Smart Environ. **2**(2), 179–195 (2010)

13. Oliveira, T., Leão, P., Novais, P., Neves, J.: Webifying the computerized execution of clinical practice guidelines. In: Perez, J.B., et al. (eds.) Trends in Practical Applications of Heterogeneous Multi-Agent Systems. The PAAMS Collection. AISC, vol. 293, pp. 149–156. Springer, Cham (2014). https://doi.org/10.1007/978-3-319-07476-4_18

14. Oliveira, T., Novais, P., Neves, J.: Representation of clinical practice guideline components in OWL. In: Pérez, J.B., et al. (eds.) Trends in Practical Applications of Agents and Multiagent Systems. AISC, vol. 221, pp. 77–85. Springer, Cham (2013). https://doi.org/10.1007/978-3-319-00563-8_10

15. Oliveira, T., Silva, A., Neves, J., Novais, P.: Decision support provided by a temporally oriented health care assistant. J. Med. Syst. **41**(1), 1–13 (2017)

16. Peleg, M.: Computer-interpretable clinical guidelines: a methodological review. J. Biomed. Inform. **46**(4), 744–63 (2013)

17. Picking, R., Robinet, A., Grout, V., McGinn, J., Roy, A., Ellis, S., Oram, D.: A case study using a methodological approach to developing user interfaces for elderly and disabled people. Comput. J. **53**(6), 842 (2010)

18. Riontech/customcalendar: Custom Android Calendar. https://github.com/Riontech/CustomCalendar

19. Shahar, Y., Miksch, S., Johnson, P.: The Asgaard project: a task-specific framework for the application and critiquing of time-oriented clinical guidelines. Artif. Intell. Med. **14**(1–2), 29–51 (1998)

20. Shalom, E., Shahar, Y., Lunenfeld, E.: An architecture for a continuous, user-driven, and data-driven application of clinical guidelines and its evaluation. J. Biomed. Inform. **59**, 130–148 (2015)

21. Silberstein, S.: Clinical practice guidelines. J. Neurosurg. Pediatr. **25**(10), 765–766 (2005)
22. Silva, A., Oliveira, T., Neves, J., Novais, P.: Transforming medical advice into clinical activities for patient follow-up. In: Bajo, J., et al. (eds.) PAAMS 2017, vol. 722, pp. 169–176. Springer, Cham (2017). https://doi.org/10.1007/978-3-319-60285-1_14
23. Terenziani, P., Montani, S., Bottrighi, A., Torchio, M., Molino, G., Correndo, G.: The GLARE approach to clinical guidelines: main features. Stud. Health Technol. Inform. **101**(3), 162–6 (2004)
24. Wang, D., Peleg, M., Tu, S.W., Boxwala, A.A., Ogunyemi, O., Zeng, Q., Greenes, R.A., Patel, V.L., Shortliffe, E.H.: Design and implementation of the GLIF3 guideline execution engine. J. Biomed. Inform. **37**(5), 305–318 (2004)
25. Young, O., Shahar, Y.: The spock system: developing a runtime application engine for hybrid-asbru guidelines. Artif. Intell. Rev. **3581**(1), 166–170 (2005)

A Multipurpose Goal Model for Personalised Digital Coaching

Jayalakshmi Baskar[1]([envelope]) [iD], Rebecka Janols[1,2], Esteban Guerrero[1] [iD],
Juan Carlos Nieves[1] [iD], and Helena Lindgren[1] [iD]

[1] Department of Computing Science, Umeå University, 901 87 Umeå, Sweden
{jayalakshmi.baskar,rebecka.janols,esteban.guerrero,
juan.carlos.nieves,helena.lindgren}@umu.se
[2] Department of Community Medicine and Rehabilitation,
Umeå University, 901 87 Umeå, Sweden

Abstract. Supporting human actors in daily living activities for improving health and wellbeing is a fundamental goal for assistive technology. The personalisation of the support provided by assistive technology in the form of digital coaching requires user models that handle potentially conflicting goals and motives. The aim of this research is to extend a motivational model implemented in an assistive technology, into a multipurpose motivational model for the human actor who is to be supported, which can be translated into a multipurpose goal model for a team of assistive agents. A team of assistive agents is outlined with supplementary goals following the human's different properties. A method for generating multipurpose arguments relating to different motives were developed, and implemented in a human-agent dialogue system. The results are exemplified based on a use case from an earlier pilot user study of the assistive technology. Future work includes user studies to validate the model.

Keywords: Personalisation · Motivation · Multiagent systems
Assistive technology · Argumentation · Persuasive technology
Behaviour change

1 Introduction

A number of systems for digital coaching have been developed for different purposes, in particular, for the purpose to increase physical exercise (e.g., [9,19,37,43]). They are typically focussed on one purpose, although the nature of humans' motivation and activity is complex [16,25,41]. Little research has been done with the aim to explore situations where multiple purposes, or goals may be relevant, and even less when different goals may be conflicting.

The purpose of the research presented in this paper is to explore multiple motives and driving forces behind human activity, and develop formal models of goals and motives as part of user modelling in order to enrich coaching for

© Springer International Publishing AG 2017
S. Montagna et al. (Eds.): A2HC 2017/A-HEALTH 2017, LNAI 10685, pp. 94–116, 2017.
https://doi.org/10.1007/978-3-319-70887-4_6

improving health and well-being. Research questions include how multiple potentially conflicting motives can be handled by a team of digital agents with different responsibilities and different knowledge domains, and how person-tailored multipurpose arguments can be composed to promote health in humans. The motive for why applying the more holistic method to generate arguments to be posed to the user is to target reasons to conduct activity that are *intrinsically* motivated, in terms of Self-Determination Theory (SDT) [41], and thereby more likely to be achieved. This way, motivation for some activities may reinforce other activities, and lead to a more sustainable behaviour change for the purpose to improve health.

The motivation for using multi-agent systems in our work is that this approach allows for modelling the conditions for reasoning and knowledge generation, in spite of ambiguous, uncertain and incomplete domain knowledge and knowledge about the user's situation. The agency of semi-autonomous software agents can be used for mixed-initiative collaborative reasoning and actions, involving also humans [42]. In addition, we anticipate that agent-based human-agent dialogues will facilitate the interaction design of more intuitive and natural dialogues between the user and the system. In particular, earlier studies with older adults (age 70 or older) participating in creating the content of digital coaching applications elicited the diverse range of trust in who or what they perceived being receiving their information [24]. We expect that the problem of transparency and trust in intelligent coaching applications that aim to support the human to change behaviour for improving health, can be addressed through clarifying the purpose of different co-operating software agents and what different sources of knowledge they utilise.

Based on humans' multiple properties and motives, we define a team of digital agents encompassing a range of goals and responsibilities to meet the needs of a human actor, which is presented in Sect. 2. A prototype mobile coaching application that aims to encourage older adults to increase their level of social and physical activity has been developed that includes a user model, which is further developed in this work into a multipurpose motivational model. The mobile application, a baseline assessment application and a dialogue application form the prototype system for personalised digital coaching, briefly introduced in Sect. 3. The proposed multipurpose motivational model is exemplified in Sect. 3.4 with a use case obtained in a user study presented in [23]. Strategies to select supporting arguments, and multipurpose arguments supporting different potentially conflicting motives are exemplified. The multipurpose motivational model is translated into a multipurpose goal model for orchestrating the personalised support by the team of agents with different goals and responsibilities, which is exemplified in Sect. 4. Related work is discussed in Sect. 5, and some conclusions and future work are summarised in Sect. 6.

2 Software Agents' Purposes, Roles and Instruments

Different roles of intelligent software agents have been targeted in research literature, e.g., *activity supporter* [2,3,21,22], *social and emotional supporter*

[10,39,54], *learning supporter* [50], *monitor of physical processes and environment* [17,21,35,38,44], *information mediator* [40] and *product promoter* [48]. Moreover, an agent may be assigned more than one role in the implementation of the different agent-based systems. A consequence of the different roles is that their motives may be in conflict, which requires that the agents have strategies to handle conflicting motives and preferences, while optimising the value of the support they provide to the human actor. In this section an analysis is presented of the different roles, which aim at proactively improving humans' health, well-being and activity performance. A summary of the roles and their properties is given in Table 1.

Our categorisation of roles of agents follows partly the functional domains of a human distinguished in the International Classification of Functioning, Disability and Health (ICF)[1], which provides an instrument for distinguishing each agent's domain of knowledge, responsibilities and prioritised goals. Another advantage is that a human actor is familiar with these domains and can relate to their different purposes, which facilitates cooperation. ICF categorises information into the following main categories: *Body Functions* and *Body Structures*, *Activity and Participation*, *Environmental Factors* (physical and social) and *Personal Factors*.

Since activity support is central to digital coaching, a generic *Activity Agent* is defined, along with activity agents targeting specific activity domains *Soc Agent*, *Bio Agent* and *Exercise Agent* (Table 1). The Activity Agent has a composite role, where for instance, the Activity Agent may be dependent on the other agents to provide the optimal support, considering the physical environment and the human actor's mental, physical and social resources. Other agents may be dedicated to focus on a subarea of another agent, such as the *Exercise Agent*, which is primarily focusing muscle strength and balance for reducing the risk for an older adult to fall. Following Activity Theory, *activity* is defined by its objective, and instruments are used for mediating the activity [25]. A *Physical Environment Agent* tracks the physical objects that are used as instruments in human activity in addition to environmental factors that affect activity such as weather and location [7].

To complement ICF, specific knowledge relating to the medical and health domains is included as instrument, utilised by agents with the role of *domain experts*. The medical and health-related qualified knowledge, which the health professionals are expected to possess, is knowledge that the human actor who is utilising the assistive technology is not expected possess, and possibly not yet the novice health professional. This knowledge is typically informally represented in medical guidelines, evidence-based medical sources, and medical terminologies and classifications. Therefore, the *Domain Expert Agent* plays a crucial role in agent-based medical decision-support systems, aiming at assisting and educating the clinician in the diagnostic procedure. Moreover, a team of domain expert agents with different domains of expertise could be useful to define for providing more reliable assessments. An important observation is that the knowledge

---

[1] http://www.who.int/classifications/icf/en/.

Table 1. The team of agents, their roles, responsibilities and examples of implementations presented in research literature.

Name	Role	Motives	Responsibilities	Reference
Companion Agent	A friend, coach or discussion partner	Guard and monitor the user's interests, prioritised goals	1. Recognise user's needs, goals, preferences; 2. Respond/act upon user's requests, needs and lack of goal satisfaction	[4,5,47,52]
Emo Agent	Monitor emotional health	Optimise positive experience and well-being	1. Recognise, evaluate emotions, experiences 2. Maximise positive emotions, experiences	[10,36]
Activity Agent	Activity supporter	Optimise activity performance	1. Recognise, evaluate activities, 2. Personalise activity support	[1,2,21,33]
Soc Agent	Monitor social environment	Organise the social resources and optimise social experience	1. Recognise, evaluate social activities 2. Maximise positive social activities	[12]
Bio Agent	Monitor physical health	Organise and optimise the body/physiological resources	1. Recognise, evaluate body signals and actions 2. Personalise support for rest vs. active life, day-night routines, food intake	[21,34,49]
Exercise Agent	Personal Trainer	Optimise strength and balance	1. Recognise, evaluate strength and balance 2. Personalise physical exercise	[2,9,19,43]
Physical Environment Agent	Monitor physical environment	Organise and optimise the tools of activity	1. Monitor the physical space and objects including the user's location 2. Personalise support for tool manipulation	[17,35,44]
Domain Expert Agent	Domain Expert	Contribute to reasoning and decision-making	Provide the expert's view on a situation	[46,53]

utilised by the Domain Expert Agent necessarily needs to be developed and validated by domain experts.

A human actor possesses resources in the following basic domains: physical, cognitive, emotional, social and environmental. Activity requires composite resources we typically call knowledge, problem solving and (motor and process) skills, partly for utilising instruments in an efficient way [26]. These resources are taken into use by the human actor in the conduction of activity and in the case of limited personal resources, a team of agents may compensate for identified limitations. However, another key to activity performance is the person's well-being, motivation, and emotional resources in a particular situation. Therefore, we define also the *Emo Agent* to elicit the particular properties required to managing the emotion and experience-related personal factors of ICF.

Finally, we add to this set of agents the *Companion Agent* that maintains the holistic perspective on the human's situation, preferences, needs and prioritised activities. In addition to these purposes, the Companion Agent may need to act as an *orchestrator* of the other agents' potential proactive behaviour, since the Companion Agent should acknowledge the human actor's current motivational status and optimise the tailored support provided the human actor. The needs and wishes of a human actor are complex and are often conflicting, which is a reason to assign the Companion Agent, this task. Moreover, it acts as the primary mediator of support from all types of agents, for not confusing, or overloading the user with information. This will be illustrated in the following sections.

To summarise, the purposes and the roles of the agents are distinguished in our approach partly by what knowledge they access, and partly, what domain of interest they should govern related to the human's activity and situation.

3   A Prototype System for Personalised Digital Coaching

The prototype system HemmaVis was developed with the aim to support older adults in planning physical and social activities, and in evaluating these (Fig. 1) [23]. Older adults include people over the age of 70 and who are at risk of social exclusion and/or falling down. This system consists of three interactive modules: (i) a baseline web application for collecting information to be fed into the initial user model (HemmaVis); (ii) a mobile application that guides in every day activities (mHemmaVis); and (iii) a web-based human-agent dialogue application for elaborating on topics related to health (NejaVis).

The content of the modules, and the structure of the baseline and mobile applications were modelled using ACKTUS, a platform for developing knowledge-based systems [32]. The platform provides a core ontology based on ICF that is used for organising information into a semantic model that distinguishes between types of motives, motivation, activities, body functions and human capabilities.

The mobile application mHemmaVis reminds the user to plan activities, encourages with messages, and the user is given feedback on their performance. The modules HemmaVis and mHemmaVis were evaluated in a formative and qualitative pilot study with four older adults, and different aspects were studied regarding how a supportive application in the form of a personalised persuasive coach could be designed to increase motivation [23]. Based on the user study and the focus groups with young and older adults, the motivational model was further extended in this work. The purpose is to develop a method for aggregating *multipurpose arguments* for the user to increase physical and social activities that are based on the user's motivation to conduct the different activities. The model is also based on theories of human motivation (SDT) [41] and on Activity Theory [25]. The formalisation of the model and implementation is built on argumentation theory [15,51].

The encouraging messages provided by mHemmaVis in the user study were the result of workshops with older adults [24]. They were designed for being generic and suitable for a range of different physical and social activities. They were also primarily designed for giving feedback as a post reflection on a day's activities. In this work, we supplement these messages with motivational person-tailored arguments, primarily aimed at encouraging the person to conduct an activity as planned. Feedback messages of a more argumentative type were created, also using ACKTUS and its ontology.

The human-agent dialogue system NejaVis provides the initial implementation of a Companion Agent that utilises such arguments, and complements the baseline assessment and the mobile application by allowing the human to select a topic to be discussed relating to his/her situation. Conclusions are collaboratively drawn through nested argumentation-based dialogues about a condition and about what to do about the situation. If there are disagreements about what to do, the agent will argue to persuade the human to follow earlier stated priorities. NejaVis uses the baseline information, but will update and extend this information during the dialogues.

In the following subsections we present the baseline assessment that generates the initial user model, and the dialogue application that implements different types of argumentation-based dialogues using tailored multipurpose arguments.

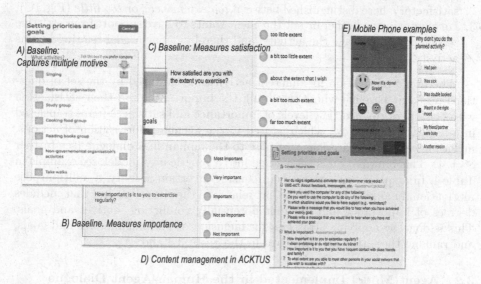

Fig. 1. Screenshots from the baseline application, the mobile application and the content management system ACKTUS.

3.1   Baseline Assessment for Creating the Motivational Model

At baseline the user provides information about how important different kinds of activities are (Fig. 1). This information forms a base for a motivational model, as an extension to the user model [23, 28, 29].

The categories of *motives* or *needs* that direct human activity, following the terminology of Activity Theory [25], are based on earlier studies involving a group of older adults [27]. These are the following:

(i) being part of, and maintaining a social network,
(ii) being part of society,
(iii) maintaining physical strength and physical health,
(iv) maintaining mental health,
(v) performing activities of one's choice,
(vi) having fun and being entertained,
(vii) feeling safe and secure.

Notably, Motives (i)–(vi) correspond to the purposes of the different agents, described in Table 1, while Motive (vii) should be a common goal for all agents. Questions about activities relating to these motives are integrated as part of the baseline assessment. The human specifies for each category of activity the following:

1. **Importance:** the degree of importance to the client following a five item scale ranging from *not important* to *most important* (Fig. 1B),
2. **Satisfaction:** to which extent the activity is currently being performed in a satisfactory way. The categories of degrees relate to satisfactory or not satisfactory, here distinguished between *too extensively*, or *too little* (Fig. 1C),
3. **Intervention:** whether or not the client wants to have support from assistive technology to manage the activity, and thereby define a goal relating to this activity.

The user's motivation for different activities is captured by the set of questions posed at baseline where they rank the importance, and their satisfaction with their performance. The levels of importance and satisfaction are translated into a measure of *weight*, which is used in the agent's prioritisation of actions, including selection of argument to pose to the human in a dialogue (see further Sect. 4). This information is aggregated into a generic user model, see example in Table 4. In a specific situation when focusing a certain activity, a multipurpose motivational model is aggregated that relates to the situation, and that includes degrees of importance and different potentially conflicting motives and goals. This is done by applying strategies for inclusion of relevant motives and goals, and ranking these (further described in the Sects. 3.4 and 4).

3.2   Agent Model Implemented in the Human-Agent Dialogue System

The agent model includes goals, priorities, responsibilities, role(s) and knowledge, which contributes to a cognitive agent architecture [4] that implements the BDI

(Belief, Desire, Intention) framework [14]. In brief, a set of *Beliefs* represents the agent's knowledge, *Desires* are the agent's goals, and *Intentions* are the agent's plans of action. The belief and desire properties of agents are described in this section, and intentions, or plans, will be briefly introduced in the following section (Sect. 3.3). The agent architecture is implemented in the human-agent dialogue system NejaVis, which functions as a module in the ACKTUS-based HemmaVis architecture, and which illustrates the Companion Agent.

A separate project for modelling the agents was created by using the ACK-TUS platform [32] including the ACKTUS core ontology, which is shared between ACKTUS applications. The agent knowledge repository was built using the ACKTUS core ontology and extended to include the different roles and social knowledge relating to the different kinds of human-agent dialogues, which is shared by the different agents. The agent-specific knowledge repository and the domain-specific knowledge bases are represented using the Resource Description Framework (RDF)[2] and Web Ontology Language (OWL)[3], and function as the common vocabulary in the dialogues.

Each instantiated agent stores its specific learnt knowledge in an *actor repository*, along with the dialogue lines. The following is an example of how the companion agent NejaVis presented in this article is defined in the actor repository:

```
<rdf:Description rdf:about="http://www.cs...na/owl-files/
    ACKTUS.owl#nejavis">
  <rdf:type rdf:resource="http://www.w3.org/2000/01/rdf-schema
    #Resource"/>
  <rdf:type rdf:resource="http://www.cs...na/owl-files/ACKTUS.
    owl#companion-agent"/>
  <ACKTUS:has-name>NejaVis</ACKTUS:has-name>
  <ACKTUS:has-role>companion-agent</ACKTUS:has-role>
</rdf:Description>
```

The agent utilises different domain-specific knowledge bases as instruments depending on its role. In the ACKTUS knowledge bases, domain expert knowledge utilised by the Domain Expert Agent is distinguished by its association to the argument scheme *Argument from Expert Opinion* [51], or more specific medical schemes. In argumentation literature the notion of *argument scheme* is applied for providing semi-formal or formal templates and defeasible inference rules for different kinds of dialogues [51]. An argumentation scheme is defined as a generic patterns of reasoning, and is instantiated by computable arguments, e.g., following the Argument Interchange Format (AIF), which is the approach taken in our research [15].

Knowledge that is considered as more generic knowledge is associated in our research to the argumentation scheme *Argument from Position to Know*. This type of knowledge is accessed by the other agents in Table 1. In addition, knowledge that is associated to the argumentation scheme *Argument from Observation* is used by the agents that take in information from wearable sensors e.g., the Bio Agent or sensors in the environment e.g., the Physical Environment Agent.

---

[2] http://www.w3.org/RDF/.
[3] http://www.w3.org/OWL/.

Consequently, several agents can access the same domain knowledge repository but each is restricted to a sub-set of the knowledge, tailored to its role. Moreover, a particular agent may have access to more than one knowledge repository. NejaVis has in the example presented in this paper access to two particular domain-specific knowledge bases: *ACKTUS-Dementia* [31] and *ACKTUS-Rehab* [30].

3.3 Personalised Digital Coaching Through Argument-Based Dialogues

Each of the five types of dialogue implemented in NejaVis has a goal in relation to the topic of a dialogue [6] (Table 2). *Information-seeking* dialogues seek new information that can be base for arguments; *inquiry* dialogues aim to generate new knowledge through conclusions about situations; *deliberation* dialogues aim to generate a plan of action to alter the situation; *persuasive* dialogues aim to change attitudes, in our approach the attitude is represented by the value, or weight a person assigns a motive or condition; and *support* dialogues aim to reinforce the human's capacity (autonomy, relatedness and competence).

Table 2. Dialogue types and their characteristics. The topic is drawn from the ACKTUS repositories, using the semantic characteristics of the knowledge nodes.

Type	Goal	Topic	Valid moves
Information-seeking	Collect information	*concept*	Open, ask, tell, affirm, close
Inquiry	Create new knowledge in the form of defeasible facts or defeasible rules	*i-node* (defeasible fact) or *s-node* (defeasible rule)	Open, assert, believe, affirm, close
Deliberation	Decide about actions to be taken	*i-node* (defeasible fact) or *s-node* (defeasible rule)	Open, assert, believe, affirm, close
Persuasion	Change a priority or belief	*i-node* (defeasible fact) or *s-node* (defeasible rule), in particular their *value* as a part of a *scale*	Open, assert, believe, affirm, remind, close
Support	Enhance human agent's ability	*information-node* or *conclusion*	Open, affirm, tell, alert, remind, close

The *topic* of a dialogue is retrieved from a domain ontology based on the ACKTUS core ontology, which incorporates both the Argument Interchange Format (AIF) [15] and the domain knowledge, structured based on primarily ICF. AIF distinguishes between *i-node*, a kind of information node, which forms statements; and *s-node* (scheme-node), from which arguments are generated.

These two types of nodes are used as topic in inquiry, deliberation and persuasion dialogues, with some differences (Table 2). In our approach an i-node is associated to a *concept* to identify the topic, and to a *value*. The formal distinction made in this approach between the inquiry and deliberation dialogues is that the *claim*, i.e., i-node, is in deliberation dialogues associated to a concept related to the ICF-node *Activity and Participation* in the domain ontology (e.g., *Taking a walk*), while in the inquiry dialogues the concept is a node different from the activity and participation branch of the ontology (e.g., *Pain condition*). Persuasive dialogues can have both kinds, since the focus is the *evaluation of* the phenomenon represented by the concept. This evaluation is represented by its *value* (e.g., status of an activity, or degree of importance of a motive), which is targeted to be changed. This can be to change the status of a planned activity from *not initiated*, to *initiated* (example about taking a walk in Table 6), or the attitude towards managing a pain condition that causes trouble in daily life from *not important* to *very important*.

i-nodes are treated as *statements* in the dialogue, and *literals* in the logic implemented in the dialogue system. Formally, we treat the i-nodes that are associated to a value as predicates of the form α. Rules extracted from the s-nodes that build the arguments, are formally defined as follows: $\alpha_1 \wedge \cdots \wedge \alpha_n \rightarrow \alpha_0$ where α_i is a literal. The rules together with defeasible facts (statements) fulfilling premises of the rules are used for building arguments of the form (G, α), where α is the claim and G is the support, or grounds for the claim, consisting of rules and facts. An argument is posed in the dialogue with an *assert* move (see examples in Table 6). In order to build arguments, it is assumed that at least one rule exists in the knowledge base for the agent to fetch during the dialogue, which has the dialogue topic or claim (α) as the conclusion. If a question posed by an *ask* move in an information-seeking dialogue gives the required answer to fulfil the premise, this new fact and the rule form the grounds (G) for the conclusion α (e.g., Fig. 2).

Attacks by the human on arguments are identified by a disagreeing response given by the human to the question posed by the agent using the *believe* move (example in Fig. 2). This disagreement is typically respected, and the agent's argument is considered defeated. However, if the human disagrees on an advice about what to do about a troublesome condition, the Companion Agent can initiate a persuasive dialogue trying to convince the human to take action, such as contacting the nurse about a pain condition. If the human supports the argument, the argument is considered accepted and validated.

The complete list of dialogue moves is presented in Table 3. Formally, a *dialogue move* for the human or software agent is a tuple (t, a, m) where t is time point of the dialogue move, a is the agent and m is the dialogue move. The *Open* move is the first action carried out to initiate a dialogue, and the *Close* move is used for closing, or stating the end of a dialogue. In our implementation, the human initiates the first dialogue, while the agent initiates all sub-dialogues. Moreover, we limit the type of dialogues to *asymmetric* dialogues, where the human is not providing own claims, only responding to questions. The *Assert*

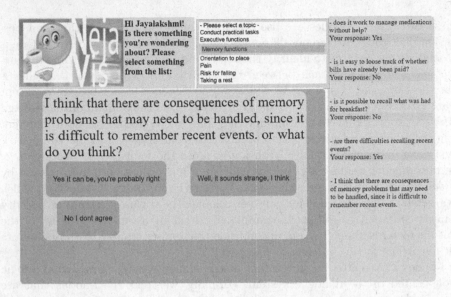

Fig. 2. Screenshot from the human-agent dialogue system (NejaVis). The topic of dialogue selected by the user is "Memory functions". The agent initiates an inquiry dialogue on the topic and after a few nested information-seeking dialogue moves, the agent poses its first argument and a *believe* move. The human can then agree or disagree to this argument as response. If the human agrees, the next step would be to initiate a deliberation dialogue to decide what to do about the situation. The dialogue line is visible on the right side.

move is used for making a claim about some topic, and it is supported by the set of grounds on which the claim is being based. The claim is a defeasible fact. The *Believe* move is a particular question posed together with an assert move for investigating if the other agent agrees upon the claim, stated in the assert move. The response is given by a tell move and can be to agree, disagree or being uncertain in our implementation (Fig. 2). In the dialogues between agents exemplified in Sect. 4, the types of moves are limited to *open*, *close* and *assert*.

A *dialogue line* is the sequence of moves conducted by the agents and their time points (e.g., [11]). The Companion Agent stores dialogue lines in its repository in order to continue at a later occasion when a dialogue may have been paused. Such sequence is visible in the examples presented in Fig. 2 and Table 6. The following is an excerpt from the actor repository, stored by companion agent during the running example shown in Fig. 2:

```
<rdf:Description rdf:about="http://www.cs...na/owl-files/
    ACKTUS.owl#event25-06-2017_13:19:00">
  <rdf:type rdf:resource="http://www.w3.org/2000/01/rdf-schema
    #Resource"/>
  <rdf:type rdf:resource="http://www.cs...na/owl-files/ACKTUS.
    owl#event_1430412506833"/>
  <ACKTUS:has-date>25-06-2017</ACKTUS:has-date>
```

```
<ACKTUS:has-start-time>13:19:00</ACKTUS:has-start-time>
<ACKTUS:has-dialogueType>infoseeking dialogue</ACKTUS:has-
    dialogueType>
<ACKTUS:has-dialogueTopic>Concept1299070752573</ACKTUS:has-
    dialogueTopic>
<ACKTUS:has-evidence>does it work to manage medications
    without help?---Yes</ACKTUS:has-evidence>

.
.
.

</rdf:Description>
```

The Agent's Planning During a Dialogue: The Companion Agent implemented in NejaVis retrieves the set of information that relates to the topic selected by the human, and creates a plan based on the human's preference order of the topics. At each step in a dialogue when receiving new information from the human, the agent analyses the information, decides whether to continue the current dialogue, pause it for opening a new sub-dialogue, or close the dialogue to possibly start a new dialogue. After this, the agent either abandons the current plan to make a new plan, or adjusts the current plan.

The content of the plan is different depending on the type of dialogue. In the case of information-seeking dialogues, the plan contains a set of questions

Table 3. Valid actions, i.e., moves and their formats. All moves contain the time identifier t_n, and the identification of the agent a_i, which performs the move.

Move	Form	Comment
Open	$(t_n, a_i, open(d_o, \alpha_m))$	d_o is the dialogue type, α_m is the topic of a dialogue
Close	$(t_n, a_i, close(d_o, \alpha_m))$	α_m is the topic of a dialogue
Ask	$(t_n, a_i, ask(CQ))$	CQ is a structured question
Affirm	$(t_n, a_i, affirm(\alpha_m))$	α_m is an expression reinforcing the previous statement
Tell	$(t_n, a_i, tell(\alpha_m))$	α_m is the message, typically an advice or information
Remind	$(t_n, a_i, remind((\alpha_m, G), a_j))$	α_m is the reminder, G is the set of reasons for the reminder, and a_j is the agent targeted for the reminder
Alert	$(t_n, a_i, alert((\alpha_m, G), a_j, t_l))$	t_l is the timeout for the action
Assert	$(t_n, a_i, assert(\alpha_m, G, (\beta, g_m)))$	α_m is the claim, G is the set of grounds for the claim, β is the weight related to the motive g_m
Believe	$(t_n, a_i, believe(\alpha_m, CQ))$	α_m is the claim or message and CQ is a structured question

(outcome is answers); in inquiry dialogues the plan contains either a set of defeasible rules or facts (outcome is arguments or new knowledge); in the case of a deliberation dialogue the plan contains a set of potential actions to be decided upon (outcome is actions agreed upon); and in the persuasion dialogues the plan contains a set of statements and arguments related to the dialogue goal, which may be used in a persuasive argumentation dialogue (outcome is a change of priority or belief).

3.4 Multipurpose Motivational Arguments

Motivational arguments for conducting a particular activity can be augmented with different weights, based on how the user rated the importance and satisfaction of the underlying motive. In the multipurpose motivational model these different arguments are used for aggregating strength for conducting a particular activity, by using the strength of arguments promoting other motives. For space reasons, we omit the potential counter-arguments *against* conducting a particular activity, e.g., Arg_{2a} in Table 5. However, in future work, these need also to be weighted, included and evaluated in the dialogues with the human, since these also affect the human's decision-making.

The generation of arguments relating to specific domains is the task of the agent that is responsible for managing activities that aim to fulfil the particular motive and related knowledge (Tables 4 and 5): the Emo Agent for Motive g_1; the Soc Agent for the second motive g_2 and the Bio Agent and Exercise Agent for Motive g_3 and its sub-goals. The Activity Agent monitors the generic every day activities that fulfil the last motive g_4. The Companion Agent coordinates the generation of multipurpose arguments.

Table 4. The generic user model for a particular person that is translated into a multipurpose motivational model for a particular activity, such as taking a walk.

g_i	Motive	Goal Rank	Importance: 0–4	Satisfaction	Motivation
g_1	Have fun, feel good	1	4: Most important	4: Too little	intrinsic
g_2	Maintain social network	1	4: Most important	4: Too little	intrinsic
g_3	Maintain physical capacity and health	3	2: Not that important	3: Bit too little	extrinsic
g_{3a}	Minimise pain	2	3: Important	4: Too little	intrinsic
g_4	Managing "musts", e.g., personal economy	3	2: Not that important	3: Bit too little	extrinsic

Multipurpose arguments are formed (examples in Table 5) that use person-specific information about the different activities (Table 4). The strength of arguments is generated based on the user's rated importance and satisfaction levels corresponding to the Goal Rank in Table 4. Optimal weight of an argument is 1. The average weight is calculated in the following examples of combining arguments into multipurpose arguments. The weight together with broad goal

Table 5. Argument examples applied to the situation to decide whether to take a walk. An argument's weight β is based on Goal Rank in Table 4, and 1 is the optimal weight.

Arg_i	Argument components	Motive g_j	β
Arg_1	G_1: *Taking walks maintains physical capability, you value maintaining physical capability as important*, therefore, α_0: *take the walk*	g_3: Maintain physical capacity and health	3
Arg_{2a}	G_2a: *It is painful to walk, therefore, not* α_0: *Do not take the walk*	g_{3a}: Minimise pain	2
Arg_{2b}	G_2: *Walking reduces pain after the walk is done, you value minimising pain as very important, therefore,* α_0: *take the walk*	g_{3a}: Minimise pain	2
Arg_3	G_3: *Taking walks maintains physical capability, you value maintaining physical capability as important, Walking reduces pain after the walk is done, you value minimising pain as very important, therefore,* α_0: *take the walk.* (Arg_1, Arg_{2b})	g_3: Maintain physical capacity and health; g_{3a}: Minimise pain	2.5
Arg_4	G_4: *Be physically active because this is the norm, you value managing "musts" as important, therefore,* α_0: *take the walk*	g_4: Managing "musts"	3
Arg_5	G_5: *Conducting activity with friends increases joy, you value having fun and feeling good as most important, therefore,* α_1: *contact a friend to join the activity*	g_1: Have fun and feel good	1
Arg_6	G_6: *Conducting activity together with others maintains social network, you value maintaining social network as most important, therefore,* α_1: *contact a friend to join the activity*	g_2: Maintain social network	1
Arg_7	G_7: *Conducting activity with friends increases joy, you value having fun and feeling good as most important, Conducting activity together with others maintains social network, you value maintaining social network as most important, therefore,* α_1: *contact a friend to join the activity*	g_1: Have fun and feel good; g_2: Maintain social network	1
Arg_8	G_8: *Conducting activity with friends increases joy, you value having fun and feeling good as most important, Conducting activity together with others maintains social network, you value maintaining social network as most important, Walking reduces pain after the walk is done, you value minimising pain as very important, therefore,* $\alpha_{0,1}$: *contact a friend to join the activity and take the walk.* (Arg_5, Arg_6, Arg_{2b})	g_1: Have fun and feel good; g_2: Maintain social network; g_{3a}: Minimise pain	1.3

satisfaction are used for evaluating arguments and to find the best argument in a persuasive dialogue with the human.

The following are three potential strategies for building arguments (Strategies 1–3 in Table 6):

1. Combine different arguments that are specifically targeting the motive that is ranked as most relevant in relation to the activity in focus,
2. Combine different arguments that are directly targeting the activity in focus regardless motive, or
3. Merge motives and generate multi-purpose arguments that are directly or indirectly targeting the activity in focus.

If the first strategy is applied in our example of taking a walk, the Companion Agent involves only the Bio Agent and Exercise Agent in the orchestration of generating optimal response. In the third approach, the Companion Agent needs to involve also the Emo Agent and Soc Agent, to be able to aggregate the multipurpose arguments that meet the human's highest ranked motives. In the following section this example is extended to involve a team of agents orchestrated by the Companion Agent.

4   Orchestrating a Team of Agents with Different Goals

In this section we outline how the Companion Agent translates the multipurpose motivational model for the human actor in a certain situation into a *multipurpose goal model* for the agent team when orchestrating the team of agents for the purpose to optimise the support to the human.

The agents' communication process to coordinate activities is based on the agent model presented in Sect. 3.2 that includes their shared *vocabulary* in the form of a formal ontology, and a set of *strategies*, or *heuristics* that the agents agree upon. The strategies regard how to collaboratively find the best action

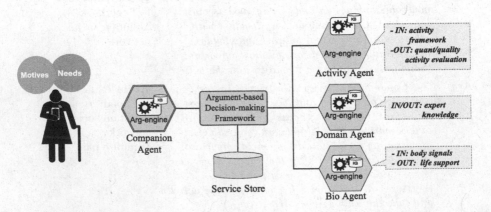

Fig. 3. Multiple agents being orchestrated by a Companion Agent.

to make in a given situation to provide support to the person. These strategies form a decision-making framework based on argumentation (Argument-based decision-making framework module in Fig. 3). In this paper, we extend the notion of deliberative argumentation dialogues introduced in [35] to centralise the decision-making process into the Companion Agent by updating goal priorities of a *commitment store CS* and by adding a *service store SS* with the selected best actions following a different ranking based on current situation. In the agent's topology shown in Fig. 3, we assume a broadcasting operation of the communications using a publish-subscribe communication pattern.

Along the entire dialogue-based communication, every agent updates their commitment stores. In this setting, the process for updating services in the *SS* is performed by the Companion Agent by re-ranking potential services according to user preferences through aggregating multipurpose arguments.

The Companion Agent (CA) initiates a deliberation dialogue (dd) with relevant agents based on the status of a planned activity item part of the plan of action that was agreed upon between the human and the Companion Agent, and that has not been initiated at a particular pre-defined time point: ⟨*Taking a walk, Today, Not initiated*⟩, associated to the motive *Maintain physical capacity and health* defined in our ontology. The dialogue follows the structure introduced in Sect. 3.3, but limits the types of moves to *open, assert* and *close*. The outcome of a dialogue that follows the first strategy introduced in Sect. 3.4, to focus only on information relevant to the motive directly associated to the activity, would unfold as the first 1–4 moves in Table 6 and end with a conclusion based on the weights of the two relevant arguments Arg_1 and Arg_2, which would be Arg_3 in Table 6.

Table 6. Example of an orchestrated dialogue where the Moves 1–4 follows Strategy 1, Move 5 is added if applying Strategy 2, and Moves 5–9 are added if Strategy 3 is applied.

t_i	Agent	Argument	Move	SS
1	CA	α_0: Taking a walk, value$_0$: Not initiated	$(t_1, a_1, open(dd_1, (\alpha_0, value_0)))$	
2	ExA	Arg_1	$(t_2, a_2, assert(G_1, \alpha_0, (3, g_3)))$	
3	BA	Arg_2	$(t_3, a_3, assert(G_2, \alpha_0, (2, g_{3a})))$	
4	CA	Arg_3	$(t_8, a_1, assert(G_3, \alpha_0, (2.5, g_3)))$	Arg_3
5	AA	Arg_4	$(t_5, a_4, assert(G_4, \alpha_0, (3, g_4)))$	Arg_3
6	EmA	Arg_5	$(t_6, a_5, assert(G_5, \alpha_1, (1, g_1)))$	
7	SA	Arg_6	$(t_7, a_6, assert(G_6, \alpha_1, (1, g_2)))$	
8	CA	Arg_7	$(t_8, a_1, assert(G_7, \alpha_1, (1, g_{1,2})))$	
9	CA	Arg_8	$(t_9, a_1, assert(G_8, \alpha_{0,1}, (1.3, g_{1-3})))$	Arg_8, Arg_3
10–14	ALL	close	$(t_6, a_{1-5}, close(dd_1, (\alpha_0, value_0)))$	

If the second strategy would be applied where the activity is in focus, then also Move 5 that targets taking a walk would be considered. However, the outcome would remain the same in our example. If the third strategy presented in Sect. 3.4 would be applied, the Companion agent would engage additional agents that contribute with arguments targeting activity at a more general level. Then the dialogue may continue with the moves 6–9 in the example in Table 6.

Consequently, the Companion Agent can aggregate multipurpose arguments using different decision-making strategies. To maximise the weight of an argument, the average needs to be as low as possible. The support for the decision to pose the recommendation to take the walk would be strongest if the argument only contains the reminder about the pain issue (weight = 2). If all grounds are applied that target the activity in focus (G_1, G_2, G_4), the weight would be 2.67 and may actually have the opposite effect on the human, i.e., decrease motivation.

If instead the strategy is to maximise the weight, then only the arguments provided by the Emo Agent and the Soc Agent would be posed to the human (weight = 1). This may shift the focus of the human from the pain condition, and the semi-motivation for exercise in general, towards something valued as significantly more important to the person. However, then the agent will loose the activity in focus as topic, and the effect may be that the person conducts a completely different activity.

Based on this analysis, the shared decision-making strategy in our approach is therefore based on that the Companion Agent follows the procedure presented in List 1, and that the other agents agree on the procedure and evaluation criteria.

Finally, as results of the orchestration process, the Companion Agent has a holistic perspective on the individual's current situation, and a ranked set of situated actions that the agent can take on behalf of the team of agents part of the multiagent system. These actions and their new ranking are stored in SS (Arg_8, Arg_3). Since Arg_5-Arg_7 are not targeting the activity in focus, these are not options stored in SS. However, by considering them as part of the deliberation dialogue, they have contributed with persuasive content to the activity in focus. Consequently, four of the five agents (CA, BiA, EmA, SoA) have contributed to selecting the best action for persuading the person to conduct the particular planned activity. In our example, the actions are persuasive arguments to motivate the human to follow though with her/his plan of actions to improve her/his health.

The Companion Agent's next step would be to select a time point suitable to remind the person about the planned activity and initiate a composite dialogue consisting of the reminder, motivating messages to support the activity initiation, and persuasion using the top ranked argument among the arguments generated by the team of agents. In case the human decides anyway to not initiate the activity as planned, an information-seeking dialogue can be initiated to investigate the reasons (could be change of attitudes, increased pain, etc.), and a deliberation dialogue to make a new plan can be conducted.

Orchestration steps (List 1): The Companion Agent's steps to orchestrate a deliberation dialogue to decide the agent's optimal next move in a persuasive dialogue with a human.

1 CA identifies the *Activity in focus* that has not been initiated as planned.
2 CA identifies the Motive behind the *Activity in focus*.
3 CA identifies the agents responsible for the *Motive*.
4 CA initiates a deliberation dialogue using an opening move:
$\langle CA, open\ (d, \langle \alpha_0, (\beta, g) \rangle) \rangle$.
5 Agents make moves targeting both *Motive* and *Activity in Focus*:
$\langle a_i, assert\ (\langle G, \alpha_j, (\beta, g) \rangle) \rangle$
6 CA merges motives and generates multi-purpose arguments targeting both *Motive* and *Activity in focus*.
7 CA evaluates the arguments based on Motive, selects the best argument and stores this in SS.
8 Additional agents contribute with arguments targeting the *Activity in focus* regardless motive: $\langle a_i, assert\ (\langle G, \alpha_j, (\beta, g) \rangle) \rangle$.
9 CA merges motives and generates multi-purpose arguments targeting the Activity in focus.
10 CA evaluates the arguments based on the *Activity in focus*, selects the best argument and stores this in SS if not stored before.
11 Additional agents contribute with arguments targeting any motive and activity at a more general level: $\langle a_i, assert\ (\langle G, \alpha_j, (\beta, g) \rangle) \rangle$.
12 CA merges motives and generates multi-purpose arguments targeting activity at a more general level.
13 CA evaluates the arguments based on the Activity in focus in combination with the most high-ranked Motives above a threshold, and stores this in SS if not stored before.
14 All agents make a close move to end the dialogue: $\langle a_{i-n}, close, (d, \langle \alpha_0, (\beta, g) \rangle) \rangle$.

5   Related Work

The coordination of teams of agents with different roles has been explored in decision making in medical contexts, e.g. regarding organ viability [46], and in ambient assisted living (AAL) (e.g. [17]). In the example of organ transplantation, the task follows treatment protocols defined for the domain to reach an optimal medical decision, and is as such constrained by the relevant medical knowledge. A moderator agent has the role of making the final decision, in case of conflicting opinions among the agents. It is not clear whether this agent is a physician, in order to assign the responsibility of the medical decision to a human. In the AAL project [17], the task to be conducted has also been primarily defined from the care provider organizations perspective, that is, to deliver certain care services, without taking a holistic perspective on the human actor's motives and goals into consideration. When addressing person-adaptive systems that aim to promote changes in behavior towards more healthy living, the holistic and situated perspective on human activity similar to what therapists aim for, is instrumental [37,41]. Along the theme to support professionals in the health domain, a multi-agent system for primarily supporting occupational therapists is presented, which includes a method to also involve the patient [13]. However, to our knowledge, there is no system that handles the complexity and uncertainty of human reasoning using agents with multiple and potentially conflicting roles, all with the purpose to adhere to the human's intentions.

Several generic platforms and methodologies for creating multi-agent systems have been developed [8,20,45]. Some of these approaches simply support the creation and interaction of agents such as JADE [8]. However, for our requirements, to develop a multi-agent system with the human as one of the actors, in the healthcare domain, key concepts such as norms, knowledge base and agent roles, are significant. The initial version of the Tropos methodology [20] was focused on supporting the agent development life cycle; however, it does not support the concept of norms. In an enhanced version of Tropos by Telang [45], commitments represent contracts between actors however, they do not establish limits on their behaviours. In addition, it is to be noted that social relationship contracts are only partially supported. Similarly, JADE allows the execution of agents in mobile devices but requires using specific libraries that are only available for certain platforms such as Android or J2ME (Java 2 Micro Edition). In addition, it lacks the support for the development of virtual organization with norms etc. Other approaches to MAS such as PANGEA [13,55] can be used for our purposes since they permit the creation of virtual organizations with key concepts such as norms and roles. However, for the purpose of prototyping, we focus on the agents modeling and development based on Java with communication based on the exchange of JSON messages between the human and software agent. Their utilization of the ACKTUS knowledge bases are also instrumental in our approach.

6   Conclusions and Future Work

A multipurpose motivational model that captures potentially conflicting motives for social and physical activity is presented. This model is used by a Companion Agent that transforms the information into a multipurpose goal model for orchestrating a team of agents with different goals and responsibilities. The agent team provides personalized support in the form of encouraging arguments tailored to the human actor's situation and motivation.

The results include also further development of the prototype application for personalized coaching. Questions were added that are posed to the user at baseline for capturing the aspects illuminated in the user studies, and feedback messages were added suitable for multipurpose arguments, following what the participants in the studies expressed.

Ongoing work includes the formalisation of the multipurpose motivational model and the agent team's goals, and implementation based on methods for formal argumentation such as answer set programming for handling the uncertainty and strengths in multipurpose arguments.

The results will be evaluated in studies with a group of older adults using the coaching application during a longer period of time.

References

1. Abel, F., Gao, Q., Houben, G.-J., Tao, K.: Analyzing user modeling on twitter for personalized news recommendations. In: Konstan, J.A., Conejo, R., Marzo, J.L., Oliver, N. (eds.) UMAP 2011. LNCS, vol. 6787, pp. 1–12. Springer, Heidelberg (2011). https://doi.org/10.1007/978-3-642-22362-4_1

2. Albaina, I.M., Visser, T., van der Mast, C.A., Vastenburg, M.H.: Flowie: a persuasive virtual coach to motivate elderly individuals to walk. In: 3rd International Conference on Pervasive Computing Technologies for Healthcare, PervasiveHealth 2009, pp. 1–7. IEEE (2009)

3. Arentze, T., Hofman, F., van Mourik, H., Timmermans, H.: Albatross: multiagent, rule-based model of activity pattern decisions. Transp. Res. Record J. Transp. Res. Board **1706**, 136–144 (2000)

4. Baskar, J., Lindgren, H.: Cognitive architecture of an agent for human-agent dialogues. In: Corchado, J.M., et al. (eds.) PAAMS 2014. CCIS, vol. 430, pp. 89–100. Springer, Cham (2014). https://doi.org/10.1007/978-3-319-07767-3_9

5. Baskar, J., Lindgren, H.: Human-agent dialogues on health topics - an evaluation study. In: Bajo, J., Hallenborg, K., Pawlewski, P., Botti, V., Sánchez-Pi, N., Duque Méndez, N.D., Lopes, F., Julian, V. (eds.) PAAMS 2015. CCIS, vol. 524, pp. 28–39. Springer, Cham (2015). https://doi.org/10.1007/978-3-319-19033-4_3

6. Baskar, J., Lindgren, H.: Human-agent dialogues and their purposes. In: Proceedings of the European Conference on Cognitive Ergonomics 2017. ECCE 2017, pp. 101–104. ACM, New York (2017). http://doi.acm.org/10.1145/3121283.3121303

7. Baskar, J., Yan, C., Lindgren, H.: Instrument-oriented approach to detecting and representing human activity for supporting executive functions and learning. In: Proceedings of the European Conference on Cognitive Ergonomics 2017. ECCE 2017, pp. 105–112. ACM, New York (2017). http://doi.acm.org/10.1145/3121283.3121305

8. Bellifemine, F.L., Caire, G., Greenwood, D.: Developing Multi-agent Systems with JADE, vol. 7. Wiley, Cambridge (2007)

9. Bickmore, T., Mauer, D., Brown, T.: Context awareness in a handheld exercise agent. Pervasive Mobile Comput. **5**(3), 226–235 (2009)

10. Bickmore, T., Mitchell, S., Jack, B., Paasche-Orlow, M.: Response to a relational agent by hospital patients with depressive symptoms. Interact. Comput. **22**(4), 289–298 (2010)

11. Black, E., Hunter, A.: An inquiry dialogue system. Auton. Agent. Multi-Agent Syst. **19**(2), 173–209 (2009)

12. Cámara, J.P., Heras, S., Botti, V.J., Julián, V.: receteame.com: a persuasive social recommendation system. In: Demazeau et al. [18], pp. 367–370

13. Casado, A., Jiménez, A., Bajo, J., Omatu, S.: Multi-agent system for occupational therapy. In: Perez, J.B., et al. (eds.) Trends in Practical Applications of Heterogeneous Multi-Agent Systems. The PAAMS Collection. AISC, vol. 293, pp. 53–60. Springer, Cham (2014). https://doi.org/10.1007/978-3-319-07476-4_7

14. Castelfranchi, C., Falcone, R.: Founding autonomy: the dialectics between (social) environment and agent's architecture and powers. In: Nickles, M., Rovatsos, M., Weiss, G. (eds.) AUTONOMY 2003. LNCS (LNAI), vol. 2969, pp. 40–54. Springer, Heidelberg (2004). https://doi.org/10.1007/978-3-540-25928-2_4

15. Chesñevar, C., McGinnis, J., Modgil, S., Rahwan, I., Reed, C., Simari, G., South, M., Vreeswijk, G., Willmott, S.: Towards an argument interchange format. Knowl. Eng. Rev. **21**, 293–316 (2006)

16. Corchado, J.M., Bajo, J., de Paz, Y., Tapia, D.I.: Intelligent environment for monitoring alzheimer patients, agent technology for health care. Decis. Support Syst. **44**, 382–396 (2008)

17. Cortés, U., Barrué, C., Martínez, A.B., Urdiales, C., Campana, F., Annicchiarico, R., Caltagirone, C.: Assistive technologies for the new generation of senior citizens: the share-it approach. IJCIH **1**(1), 35–65 (2010)

18. Demazeau, Y., Zambonelli, F., Corchado, J.M., Bajo, J. (eds.): PAAMS 2014. LNCS (LNAI), vol. 8473. Springer, Cham (2014). https://doi.org/10.1007/978-3-319-07551-8

19. Fasola, J., Matarić, M.J.: A socially assistive robot exercise coach for the elderly. J. Hum.-Robot Interact. **2**(2), 3–32 (2013)

20. Giorgini, P., Kolp, M., Mylopoulos, J., Pistore, M.: The tropos methodology. In: Bergenti, F., Gleizes, M.P., Zàmbonelli, F. (eds.) Methodologies and Software Engineering for Agent Systems, vol. 11, pp. 89–106. Springer, Boston (2004). https://doi.org/10.1007/1-4020-8058-1_7

21. Guerrero, E., Nieves, J.C., Lindgren, H.: ALI: an assisted living system for persons with mild cognitive impairment. In: 2013 IEEE 26th International Symposium on Computer-Based Medical Systems (CBMS), pp. 526–527 (2013)

22. Hanke, S., Sandner, E., Stainer-Hochgatterer, A., Tsiourti, C., Braun, A.: The technical specification and architecture of a virtual support partner. In: Am I (Workshops/Posters) (2015)

23. Janols, R., Guerrero, E., Lindgren, H.: A pilot study on personalised coaching to increase older adults' physical and social activities. In: De Paz, J.F., Julián, V., Villarrubia, G., Marreiros, G., Novais, P. (eds.) ISAmI 2017. AISC, vol. 615, pp. 140–148. Springer, Cham (2017). https://doi.org/10.1007/978-3-319-61118-1_18

24. Janols, R., Lindgren, H.: A Study on Motivational Messages for Supporting Seniors, UMINF 17.08, Umeå University (2017)

25. Kaptelinin, V., Nardi, B.A.: Acting with Technology: Activity Theory and Interaction Design. The MIT Press, Cambridge (2006)

26. Kielhofner, G.: A Model of Human Occupation. Lippincott, Williams & Wilkins, New York (2008)

27. Lindgren, H.: Personalisation of internet-mediated activity support systems in the rehabilitation of older adults - a pilot study. In: AIME workshop on Personalisation for E-Health 2009, pp. 22–27 (2009)

28. Lindgren, H., Baskar, J., Guerrero, E., Nieves, J.C., Nilsson, I., Yan, C.: Computer-supported assessment for tailoring assistive technology. In: Proceedings of the 6th International Conference on Digital Health Conference, DH 2016, pp. 1–10 (2016)

29. Lindgren, H., Guerrero, E., Janols, R.: Personalised persuasive coaching to increase older adults' physical and social activities: a motivational model. In: Demazeau, Y., Davidsson, P., Bajo, J., Vale, Z. (eds.) PAAMS 2017. LNCS (LNAI), vol. 10349, pp. 170–182. Springer, Cham (2017). https://doi.org/10.1007/978-3-319-59930-4_14

30. Lindgren, H., Nilsson, I.: Towards user-authored agent dialogues for assessment in personalised ambient assisted living. Int. J. Web Eng. Technol. **8**(2), 154–176 (2013)

31. Lindgren, H., Winnberg, P.: Evaluation of a semantic web application for collaborative knowledge building in the dementia domain. In: Szomszor, M., Kostkova, P. (eds.) eHealth 2010. LNICSSITE, vol. 69, pp. 62–69. Springer, Heidelberg (2011). https://doi.org/10.1007/978-3-642-23635-8_8

32. Lindgren, H., Yan, C.: ACKTUS: a platform for developing personalized support systems in the health domain. In: Proceedings of the 5th International Conference on Digital Health 2015, DH 2015, pp. 135–142 (2015)

33. Liu, J., Dolan, P., Pedersen, E.R.: Personalized news recommendation based on click behavior. In: IUI, pp. 31–40 (2010)
34. Monkaresi, H., Calvo, R., Pardo, A., Chow, K., Mullan, B., Lam, M., Twigg, S., Cook, D.: Intelligent diabetes lifestyle coach. In: OzCHI Workshops Programme (2013)
35. Nieves, J.C., Lindgren, H.: Deliberative argumentation for service provision in smart environments. In: Bulling, N. (ed.) EUMAS 2014. LNCS (LNAI), vol. 8953, pp. 388–397. Springer, Cham (2015). https://doi.org/10.1007/978-3-319-17130-2_27
36. Ochs, M., Pelachaud, C., Sadek, D.: An empathic virtual dialog agent to improve human-machine interaction. In: AAMAS 2008 Proceedings of the 7th International Joint Conference on Autonomous Agents and Multiagent Systems, vol. 1, pp. 89–96 (2008)
37. op den Akker, H., Jones, V.M., Hermens, H.J.: Tailoring real-time physical activity coaching systems: a literature survey and model. User Model. User-Adap. Inter. 24(5), 351–392 (2014)
38. Reichherzer, T., Satterfield, S., Belitsos, J., Chudzynski, J., Watson, L.: An agent-based architecture for sensor data collection and reasoning in smart home environments for independent living. In: Khoury, R., Drummond, C. (eds.) AI 2016. LNCS (LNAI), vol. 9673, pp. 15–20. Springer, Cham (2016). https://doi.org/10.1007/978-3-319-34111-8_2
39. Ring, L., Shi, L., Totzke, K., Bickmore, T.: Social support agents for older adults: longitudinal affective computing in the home. J. Multimodal User Interfaces 9(1), 79–88 (2015)
40. Ruta, M., Scioscia, F., Loseto, G., Di Sciascio, E.: Semantic-based resource discovery and orchestration in home and building automation: a multi-agent approach. IEEE Trans. Industr. Inf. 10(1), 730–741 (2014)
41. Ryan, R.M., Deci, E.L.: Self-determination theory and the facilitation of intrinsic motivation, social development, and well-being. Am. Psychol. 55(1), 68–78 (2000)
42. Sanchis, A., Julián, V., Corchado, J.M., Billhardt, H., Carrascosa, C.: Improving human-agent immersion using natural interfaces and CBR. Int. J. Artif. Intell. 13(1), 81–93 (2015)
43. Sandlund, M., Lindgren, H., Pohl, P., Melander-Wikman, A., Bergvall-Kåreborn, B., Lundin-Olsson, L.: Towards a mobile exercise application to prevent falls: a Participatory Design Process. Int. J. Child Health Hum. Dev. 9(3), 389–398 (2016)
44. Surie, D., Berker, B., Lindgren, H.: Proxemics Awareness in kitchen AS-A-PAL: tracking objects and human in perspective. In: 9th International Conference on Intelligent Environments, Athens, Greece (IE 2013), pp. 157–164. IEEE Computer Society Press (2013)
45. Telang, P.R., Singh, M.P.: Enhancing tropos with commitments. In: Borgida, A.T., Chaudhri, V.K., Giorgini, P., Yu, E.S. (eds.) Conceptual Modeling: Foundations and Applications. LNCS, vol. 5600, pp. 417–435. Springer, Heidelberg (2009). https://doi.org/10.1007/978-3-642-02463-4_22
46. Tolchinsky, P., Cortes, U., Modgil, S., Caballero, F., Lopez-Navidad, A.: Increasing human-organ transplant availability: argumentation-based agent deliberation. IEEE Intell. Syst. 21(6), 30–37 (2006)
47. Tsiourti, C., Ben-Moussa, M., Quintas, J., Loke, B., Jochem, I., Lopes, J.A., et al.: A virtual assistive companion for older adults: design implications for a real-world application. In: SAI Intelligent Systems Conference (2016)
48. Vahidov, R., Kersten, G., Saade, R.: An experimental study of software agent negotiations with humans. Decis. Support Syst. 66, 135–145 (2014)

49. Vermeulen, J., Neyens, J.C., Spreeuwenberg, M.D., van Rossum, E., Sipers, W., Habets, H., Hewson, D.J., De Witte, L.P.: User-centered development and testing of a monitoring system that provides feedback regarding physical functioning to elderly people. Patient Prefer. Adherence **7**, 843 (2013)

50. Villarica, R., Richards, D.: Intelligent and empathic agent to support student learning in virtual worlds. In: Proceedings of the 2014 Conference on Interactive Entertainment, pp. 1–9. ACM (2014)

51. Walton, D., Reed, C., Macagno, F.: Argumentation Schemes. Cambridge University Press, Cambridge (2008)

52. Yaghoubzadeh, R., Kramer, M., Pitsch, K., Kopp, S.: Virtual agents as daily assistants for elderly or cognitively impaired people. In: Aylett, R., Krenn, B., Pelachaud, C., Shimodaira, H. (eds.) IVA 2013. LNCS (LNAI), vol. 8108, pp. 79–91. Springer, Heidelberg (2013). https://doi.org/10.1007/978-3-642-40415-3_7

53. Yan, C., Nieves, J.C., Lindgren, H.: A multi-agent system for nested inquiry dialogues. In: Demazeau et al. [18], pp. 303–314

54. Yu, X., Salmon, C.T., Leung, C.: Emotional interactions between artificial companion agents and the elderly. In: Proceedings of the 2015 International Conference on Autonomous Agents and Multiagent Systems, pp. 1991–1992. International Foundation for Autonomous Agents and Multiagent Systems (2015)

55. Zato, C., et al.: PANGEA – platform for automatic construction of organizations of intelligent agents. In: Omatu, S., De Paz Santana, J., González, S., Molina, J., Bernardos, A., Rodríguez, J. (eds.) Distributed Computing and Artificial Intelligence. AISC, vol. 151, pp. 229–239. Springer, Heidelberg (2012). https://doi.org/10.1007/978-3-642-28765-7_27

Prediction Models for Health and Societal Challenges

Towards Social Care Prediction Services Aided by Multi-agent Systems

Emilio Serrano(✉) and Javier Bajo

Ontology Engineering Group, Universidad Politécnica de Madrid, Madrid, Spain
{emilioserra,jbajo}@fi.upm.es

Abstract. Prediction models are widely used in insurance companies and health services. Even when 120 million people are at risk of suffering poverty or social exclusion in the EU, this kind of models are surprisingly unusual in the field of social services. A fundamental reason for this gap is the difficulty in labeling and annotating social services data. Conditions such as social exclusion require a case-by-case debate. This paper presents a multi-agent architecture that combines semantic web technologies, exploratory data analysis techniques, and supervised machine learning methods. The architecture offers a holistic view of the main challenges involved in labeling data and generating prediction models for social services. Moreover, the proposal discusses to what extent these tasks may be automated by intelligent agents.

Keywords: Multi-agent systems · Human-agent societies
Social services · Machine learning

1 Introduction

Building artificial intelligence and machine learning based systems has never been easier than today thanks to: (1) open-source tools such as TensorFlow or Spark; and, (2) massive amounts of computation power through cloud providers such as Amazon Web Services and Google Cloud [4]. Machine learning prediction models are widely employed, among others, in health services. These systems have a deep impact because there is strong evidence supporting that early detection of medical conditions results in less severe outcomes. For instance, the reader may calculate the risk of suffering a heart disease at different webs [3].

Social services, also called welfare services or social work, include publicly or privately provided services intended to aid disadvantaged, distressed, or vulnerable persons or groups. The economic crisis is undermining the sustainability of social protection systems in the EU [1]: 24% of all the EU population (over 120 million people) are at risk of poverty or social exclusion. The fight against poverty and social exclusion is at the heart of the Europe 2020 strategy for smart, sustainable and inclusive growth. Social services deal with a number of undesirable conditions that affect not only the quality of life of individuals, but also the equity and cohesion of society as a whole [10].

© Springer International Publishing AG 2017
S. Montagna et al. (Eds.): A2HC 2017/A-HEALTH 2017, LNAI 10685, pp. 119–130, 2017.
https://doi.org/10.1007/978-3-319-70887-4_7

Why not producing prediction models for the field of social services as in health services?. Machine learning could answer a number of questions such as: will this individual suffer chronic social exclusion?; will generational transmission of poverty occurs in this family?; how much economic aid is needed to integrate this person into society?; how long does it take aid to have an impact on a case?. Something that may go unnoticed by outsiders to the field of data science is that all these questions are forms of *supervised learning*. Therefore, these questions fall into two broad categories: (1) *classification* ("is this A or B?", or "is this A or B, or C...?"); and (2) *regression* (questions answered with a number: "how much", "how many", "how long").

Unsupervised learning and reinforcement learning achieve outstanding results when applicable, but they are not adequate to answer these questions. On the other hand, supervised learning is based on the premise that lots and lots of labeled and annotated data is available. There are a number of challenges in gathering this labeled data in social services. (1) There is not public and accepted datasets in the field, typically because of privacy reasons. (2) Even if there were such data, the labels to predict would not correspond to the needs of all social services because there is a strong coupling between the predictive tool and the data it is fed with. (3) Moreover, the conditions social services are concerned about depend on the society they deal with, not allowing prediction results to be extrapolated from a country or even a city to another one. (4) Finally, the complex and multi-dimensional nature of processes such as social exclusion may require a case-by-case debate and deciding a label is complicated even for social workers experts.

For the reasons explained above, the hardest part of building new artificial intelligence solutions for social services is not the machine learning algorithms, but the data collection and labeling. This paper copes with this problem by a multi-agent architecture that combines semantic web technologies, exploratory data analysis techniques, and supervised machine learning methods. The architecture is composed of a number of cooperating intelligent agents that assist social workers and data scientists in the labeling of sensitive data and in the subsequent generation of prediction services.

The rest of the paper is organized as follows: Sect. 2 revises the related work. Section 3 presents the proposed architecture, Sect. 4 details a use case for generating a prediction service, and Sect. 5 discusses the suitability of the multi-agent systems paradigm. Finally, the preliminary conclusions obtained are presented in Sect. 6. This paper extends the author's former contribution [16].

2   Related Works

Predictions models are widely used in insurance companies to allow customers to estimate their policies cost. Manulife Philippines [2] offers a number of online tools to calculate the likelihood of disability, critical illness, or death before the age of 65; based on age, gender, and smoking status. Health is another application field where risk estimations are undertaken for preventive purposes.

More specifically, the risk of heart disease can be estimated at different websites such as at the Mayo clinic web [3]. The labeling of these cases is relatively simple a posteriori: roughly speaking there is no doubt when someone has suffered one of these conditions. There are also a few online tools that social services may use for early detection. In this manner, Rank and Hirschl [15] give an online calculator that evaluates the probability of experiencing poverty in the next 5, 10 or 15 years. Labeling poverty cases is something automatic when defined as falling below a certain annual income[1].

The multi-dimensional nature of conditions such as social exclusion makes considerably more challenging to analyze, detect, treat, and predict it than poverty. There are a number of data analysis works in social exclusion that are detailed enough to learn from their labeling methods for the presented work. Ramos and Valera [14] use the *logistic regression* (LR) model to study social exclusion in 384 cases labeled by social workers through a manual heuristic procedure. According to this procedure, an individual is considered at a consolidated phase of exclusion if: (1) he or she is living for at least 3 years in unstable accommodation; (2) has very weak links, or none at all, with family or friends; (3) is almost permanently unoccupied; and, (4) presents a substantial or total loss of working habits, self-care or motivation for inclusion. Similar conditions are defined for the initial phase of exclusion. This example of rule of thump used by the social workers illustrates the complexity and ambiguity of deciding if someone is suffering social exclusion. Moreover, the heuristic has to be define before starting gathering data so the social workers can use it. Finally, the fully manual approach only allows a very limited number of cases: less than 400. Lafuente-Lechuga and Faura-Martínez [9] undertake an analysis of 31 predictors based on segmentation methods and LR. The authors consider the aggregation of scores in different fields related to social exclusion to decide if a person is under this condition. After a cluster analysis, this score is used to rank and analyze the most important variables to decide whether there is vulnerability to social exclusion. In a similar style, Haron [6] studies the social exclusion in Israel labeling data by various indicators that are aggregated in a single weighted average score. The author proposes the *linear regression* as a better alternative to the LR. The problem with this approach is that, besides the difficulty in defining these aggregations functions and weights, the machine learning techniques will tend to calculate precisely the aggregation formula since it is defined based exclusively on the training data. Suh et al. [19] analyze over 35K cases of 34 European countries using LR. The particular objective of this work is a subjective study and not an objective measure of the social exclusion, for which the researchers use LR over responses to a survey of direct questions about whether people feel excluded from society. Therefore, as the authors point out, there is a subjectivity aspect that is the responsibility of the interviewee instead of the social worker

---

[1] In this vein, the adult dataset [8] is a well known public labeled dataset that allows predicting whether an adult income exceeds $50K a year based on a 1994 census database. It can be used to train prediction models as a proof of concept before collecting and labeling the own proprietary data.

expert. These inspiring works support the hypothesis that machine learning can greatly benefit social services. Also, that the most interesting questions to assist social services belong to the supervised learning. However, there are no general methods and tools proposed for labeling the data before building a predictive model.

A number of approaches study interesting synergies between agent theory and machine learning [18]. Ponni and Shunmuganathan [13] propose multi-agent system for classification in multi-relational databases with, among others, Support Vector Machines (SVM). Kiselev and Alhajj [7] describe an efficient adaptive multi-agent approach to continuous online clustering of streaming data in complex uncertain environments. Giannella et al. [5] propose an implementation of distributed clustering algorithms with multi-agent systems. Park and Oh [12] introduce a multi-agent system to filter data that automatically selects and tunes a clustering or dimensionality reduction method. These significant contributions improve machine learning paradigms in a number of aspects by rethinking them from the perspective of multi-agent systems. More importantly for the work presented here, several of these references deal with exploratory data analysis techniques such as clustering and dimensionality reduction. These are natural solutions to summarize, simplify, condense, and distill a collection of data before labeling it. However, the revised multi-agent systems do not offer specific guidelines to go from the clusters or the principal components to the wanted labels. Clusters are in the eye of the beholder, and the architecture presented in this paper instead of focusing on implementing faster clustering techniques, is meant to adapt to the beholder and to recommend actions to label data intuitively.

3   Multi-agent Architecture Segmentation and Prediction

This section describes the proposed architecture, see Fig. 1.

In the lower layer of the architecture, there is an interface that allows accessing the databases that are used for the different applications and records in social services and linking them with the rest of the architecture. The agents of this layer, besides controlling the protocols of access to the databases, will ensure that the information that the upper layers obtain is anonymous. Users with special privileges may require this layer, through services in upper layers and with the purpose of labeling a case, to link an anonymous identifier with an identity.

The data handled by the interface are also accessed by a layer of persistence transverse to the architecture. This persistence layer has capacities of semantic technologies as dealing with ontologies in languages such as RDFS and OWL. To favor the tagging service, the architecture offers functionality for the formal representation of the knowledge treated by social services through a network of ontologies. In addition to these ontologies, the layer stores intermediate data such as: data tables obtained from pre-processing the databases accessed by the interface, unsupervised learning models, supervised learning models, and users' preferences and history of decisions for recommendation and decision support.

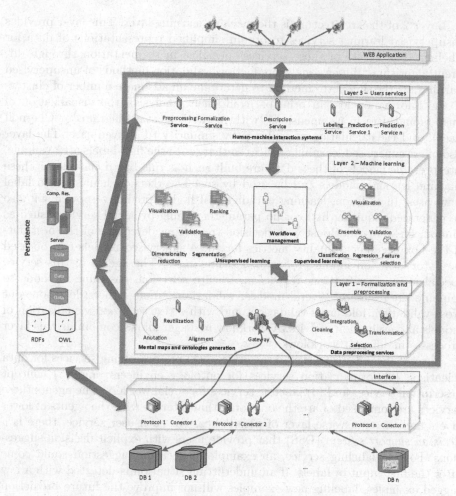

Fig. 1. A multi-agent architecture for labeling data and generating prediction models.

Layer 1 of the architecture is devoted to the formalization and preprocessing of social services data, on the one hand, to have a powerful query model based on semantic technologies and, on the other hand, to allow the machine learning methods to learn from this data. These two differentiated services are connected through a gateway: data processing services and ontology construction. The first service includes agents specialized in: (1) data selection; (2) its integration from various sources accessed by the interface; (3) cleaning the data by detecting noise and inconsistencies; (4) and, transforming the data into forms suitable for mining. The agents in charge of assisting the process of generating mental maps and ontologies are specialized in tasks such as: (1) data annotation; (2) reuse of already built ontologies; and, (3) ontology alignment, i.e. determining correspondences between concepts in ontologies.

Layer 2 of the architecture is the machine learning layer. This layer provides unsupervised learning services to obtain simplified representations of data for labeling. The agents of these services specialize in segmentation through different algorithms, dimensionality reduction, validation methods of unsupervised learning (as the silhouette method to determine an adequate number of clusters or the information loss in principal component analysis), the visualization of clusters and data in n-dimensions (with methods as star diagrams or Chernoff faces), and the calculation of rankings by similarity to a given case. The layer also offers supervised learning services so that, once the first labels are available, interpretable models of these data are built such as rule-based classifiers. These machine learning models can be used by social workers as heuristics to label new cases. In addition, learning paradigms of higher predictive power will also be generated requiring little or no parameter tuning by social services, such as random forest or AdaBoost with decision trees (considered one of the best out-of-the-box classifier). Quality metrics for these supervised models can be used as a stop criterion in the process of labeling cases. The agents of this service specialize in: classification, regression, feature selection, ensemble methods to combine the results of several models, validation (among others: leave-one-out cross-validation, fold cross-validation, and with a test set), and visualization of models and evaluation metrics. A workflow manager allows combining this layer processes in different workflows.

Layer 3 offers distinguished user services: (1) pre-processing services for data scientists; (2) formalization services for ontology engineers; and (3) concept description services and (4) labeling services for social workers. The agents these services are composed of are the only ones that interact with the agents of lower layers and the transverse layer of persistence. For each user service, there is a *decision support system* (DSS) that provide users with explicit decision suggestions. For the labeling service, an example of decision suggestion could come after the first input of labels. If an underfitting situation is detected with a few tagged examples, labeling new examples will not improve the future prediction model. In this case, some suggestions include: (1) revising the labels that might be inconsistent; (2) collecting more fields for the cases; (3) or, considering changing the purpose of the prediction model. On the other hand, if a high accuracy is achieved with the currently labeled data (or it does not improve in many iterations), stopping the labeling process could also be suggested. Finally, these services agents have to learn from the users' preferences and recommend actions and alternatives through techniques as *collaborative filtering*. Once again, clusters are in the eye and there are no inherently better cluster analysis methods than others.

In the top layer, user services are accessed through responsive web applications. In this way, users can use these services through a variety of devices: smartphones, tablets, laptops, etcetera. The ultimate goal is to provide social workers with intelligent prediction models in the palm of the hand, which allow them to anticipate events for the sake of their "social patients". But as discussed, the hardest part to get there is labeling the data.

4 Use Case

This section presents a use case for the proposed architecture with the purpose of illustrating the tasks and activities to be performed in the generation of a prediction model based on social services data. As described below, the more iterations over unlabeled data and the more prediction services are generated, the more autonomous and proactive behavior is held by the agents, getting further from a Data Science framework as RapidMiner[2] or TensorFlow[3].

Consider an intelligent service for the prediction of a social condition y. As explained in the introduction, some examples might be generational transmission of poverty, chronicity of social exclusion, or poverty. Social services experts may indicate in the pre-processing service the cases of the database that will be used to build the service, i.e. m cases composed of n independent variables $x_1, x_2...x_n$.

Agents of Layer 1, formalization and preprocessing, can undertake a series of tasks automatically and proactively once the experts have provided that information. Among others, agents in charge of pre-processing should eliminate outliers, standardize numerical values, discard variables with high percentages of unknown values, etcetera. The agents in charge of the formalization have to map the names of the variables to ontological information stored in the persistence layer or available online in order to give extended explanations of the concepts in the databases. This information can also be used by preprocessing agents to point out and remove possible redundancies in the data; or to transform nominal values into ordinals, allowing machine learning paradigms to generalize better. While these tasks typically need to be supervised by humans, agents could proactively conduct them and submit an acceptance report to the expert.

With the data generated in Layer 1, the non-supervised learning agents of Layer 2 can apply a clustering method based on the calculation of real representatives, such as *Further first* or *K-medioids*, with a reduced number of clusters, say 10. Figure 2 shows an example of K-medioids execution with $K = 2$ compared to the use of K-means over the same data. As shown, K-medioids generates

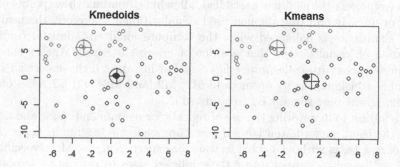

Fig. 2. Illustration of K-means vs. K-medioids.

---

[2] https://rapidminer.com/.

[3] https://www.tensorflow.org/.

cluster representatives that correspond to real cases in the data while K-means generate prototypes not included in the database. These algorithms are computationally very costly and agents must be able to change their behavior to achieve the desired goal: to obtain a reduced number, 10 in the example, of representatives of the studied cases. Some behavioral changes may include modify the distance measure to a more efficient one, load balancing calculations, splitting the input data between different agents to obtain representatives of each partition, or reducing the number of clusters to obtain. While some of these measures may mean a loss of precision in obtaining a good summary of the data, but the summary is just a starting point for initiating discussion of labeling.

The labeling service will present the 10 selected cases to the experts for discussion. In conditions such as poverty, the labeling process might end quickly by identifying a variable or an aggregate of several dimensions with a simple rule, for example ``if annual income $\geq$ 22K, then y = No''. On the other hand, many conditions such as social exclusion are much more subtle and may require a case by case debate. The description service can be used for querying extra information and disambiguating terms. According to the number of variables and their possible values, the Layer 2 agents may report for their study: a hierarchical clustering *dendrogram* to compare the similarity between the representatives (so that if one receives a label, the most similar cases could, but not necessarily, receive similar labels); multi-dimensional visualizations (such as *Chernoff faces* or Star diagrams); plots of the two or three most important variables obtained after a dimensionality reduction process if they are reasonably representative of all dimensions considered, etcetera. In a prediction service of the chronicity of social exclusion built with the ideas presented here [17], 63 variables were considered, hence labeling a few cases was very complex because of the number of dimensions to be studied.

The use of the labeling service by the experts and the study of the reports presented will provide the agents with valuable information for the following iterations of the labeling process. In this way, if the experts' profile information is available, the supervised learning agents will be able to look for patterns in the preferences in the summaries studied, allowing extending those points of the report or directly omitting the non used visualizations. Therefore, the usability of the summaries is enhanced while the computational cost derived from the generation of visualizations that are not of interest is saved. Agents can also learn preferences with *collaborative filtering*. For instance, if the expert E1 bases her or his decisions heavily on method M1, M2, and M3; and E2 relies on M1 and M2; agents may suggest E2 to study M3.

In addition to monitoring the use of reports for recommendations and adapting to the user, once the ten labeled cases are available, agents in Layer 2 can conduct new tasks without having to wait for expert requests. More specifically, supervised learning agents can use these labeled cases to generate a hypothesis that predicts the condition y based on the predictor variables $x_1, x_2...x_n$ and present it in the reports to the experts. Methods such as *One Rule* or *C4.5* offer very interpretable outputs. The agents can consult with the experts a good metric of quality of service (accuracy, recall, precision, or others) in order to optimize that metric in the calculation of the models. Nonetheless, even with poor results in the predictions, these models are an excellent manner of summarizing the formerly labeled cases to discuss new individuals diagnostics. Likewise, reports in subsequent iterations will be enriched with rankings of the most important variables to predict y with the available information, or with the subset of most relevant variables. *Feature selection* techniques such as InfoGain or Correlation based Feature Selection (CFS) allow agents to achieve this goal.

The next iteration tasks will depend on the quality metrics for the predictive model of the previous iteration and can be decided by the agents without human intervention. Supervised learning agents use powerful meta-classifiers such as *Random Forest* or *AdaBoost* on the ten labeled cases. As explained, if the validation curves show an underfitting situation, experts will be informed that the process should stopped. The given labels may be inconsistent or there is no correlation between the predictor variables and the response variable. On the other hand, an overfitting situation requires the agents to iterate in the labeling process. For this purpose, the agents may select a value of K greater than the previous iteration for the calculation of representatives through clustering. In this way, different representatives can be obtained than those used in the previous iteration, since removing the studied cases and repeating the cluster analysis would obtain very similar representatives. Experts can also be offered the option of labeling the most similar or most different cases to the representatives of the previous iteration. In addition, an overfitting situation can be improved by removing variables used and selected by the previously described methods, and at the same time the labeling process is simplified by reducing the number of dimensions to be considered for each case.

Finally, if the validation curves show a good balance between underfitting and overfitting as well as an acceptable prediction quality, agents can start labeling cases with the prediction model and include these cases in the reports, or only the most doubtful cases based on the prediction certainty. To this end, agents can seek to maximize *precision* instead of *accuracy* so that when a positive case is found, they are very sure that the case does not belong to another class.

5 Discussion: Why Agents?

The last KDnuggets Software Poll[4] collects votes for the use of 94 data science software tools. Plenty of these frameworks are capable of doing the tasks described in the use case. Why is this work innovative and why are agents suitable?

Firstly, the coverage of the architecture presented here is specific: the main objective is the labeling of data relating to social services. Focusing on the labeling is innovative because the frameworks start from the fact that labels are already available, leaving a great gap in the generation of predictive models.

---

[4] https://goo.gl/WPZtaA.

Moreover, considering the specific domain of social services, the process of labeling can be enriched with expert knowledge in the form of ontologies networks that can be consulted by humans and agents.

The main motivation of framing the proposal in the multi-agent paradigm is that, unlike in the typical data science frameworks, this architecture intends that agents perform many of the necessary tasks without requiring the call by human experts in an autonomous and proactive manner. Agents are able to exhibit goal-directed behavior by taking the initiative in order to satisfy their design objectives [20]. As seen in the use case, agents take the initiative at various points, highlighting the flow control of the iterations in the labeling process and the interactions with the experts. The social ability is also a factor of great importance since agents must adapt to the experts and present them with reports that are useful. Furthermore, dialogues and negotiations between agents may be necessary to elucidate discussions on labels based on different models. Although this process is classically undertaken by voting (as in random forest) or the use of metaclasifiers (as in *stacking*), agent languages can contribute in the domain of social sciences where the explanation of the prediction is as important as the prediction itself. Therefore, the minimum characteristics for the intelligent agents established by Nwana [11]: they are autonomous, they cooperate, and they learn; are of great use in the proposed architecture.

6   Conclusion and Future Works

This paper presents a multi-agent architecture for labeling data and generating social services prediction models. The proposal responds to the enormous importance of social services in today's Europe and to the difficulty of generating predictive models that help social workers in their day-to-day work. To improve this situation, the architecture supports an iterative and incremental data labeling until a predictive model that attends a specific social service is obtained.

The core of the proposal is based on offering services and assistance to social workers in cluster analysis and dimensionality reduction as a means to summarize, simplify, condense, and distill a collection of data before labeling it. Intelligent agents not only automate this analysis as much as possible, but also learn from workers' preferences since there is a lack of objectivity in the generation of useful summaries and visualizations of unlabeled data. Furthermore, the architecture includes agents for supervised learning that, in each iteration in which new labels are added, contribute with: explanatory models of the data; selections of the most important predictors; and, stopping conditions to the labeling process automatically checked. Finally, it provides a service for the consultation of ontology networks that facilitates the unambiguous description of the concepts included in the cases to be tagged and their relations.

Although the architecture has not been implemented, many of the ideas and proposals have been put into practice for the generation of an online social exclusion prediction service in the Spanish region of Castilla y León [17].

Future work includes: implementing the architecture in a multi-agent platform; extending the decision support system for the labeling service; considering different machine learning problems as multi-instance learning and multi-label learning; and, a better exploitation of the ontologies and semantic resources to include forms of advanced learning such as case-based reasoning, transfer learning, and graph mining.

Acknowledgments. This research work is supported by the Spanish Ministry of Economy, Industry and Competitiveness under the R&D project Datos 4.0: Retos y soluciones (TIN2016-78011-C4-4-R, AEI/FEDER, UE).

References

1. European Commission's DG for Employment, Social Affairs & Inclusion. http://ec.europa.eu/social/main.jsp?catId=751. Accessed Feb 2017
2. Manulife Philippines. Calculate your risk, your partner's risk or both. http://www.insureright.ca/what-is-your-risk. Accessed Feb 2017
3. Mayo Clinic. Heart Disease Risk Calculator. http://www.mayoclinic.org/diseases-conditions/heart-disease/in-depth/heart-disease-risk/itt-20084942. Accessed Feb 2017
4. de Oliveira, L.: Fueling the Gold Rush: The Greatest Public Datasets for AI. https://goo.gl/mJO8nf. Accessed Feb 2017
5. Giannella, C., Bhargava, R., Kargupta, H.: Multi-agent systems and distributed data mining. In: Klusch, M., Ossowski, S., Kashyap, V., Unland, R. (eds.) CIA 2004. LNCS (LNAI), vol. 3191, pp. 1–15. Springer, Heidelberg (2004). https://doi.org/10.1007/978-3-540-30104-2_1
6. Haron, N.: Poverty and social exclusion around the mediterranean sea. In: Berenger, V., Bresson, F. (eds.) On social exclusion and income poverty in Israel: findings from the European social survey. Economic Studies in Inequality, Social Exclusion and Well-Being, vol. 9, pp. 247–269. Springer, Boston (2013). https://doi.org/10.1007/978-1-4614-5263-8_9
7. Kiselev, I., Alhajj, R.: A self-organizing multi-agent system for adaptive continuous unsupervised learning in complex uncertain environments. In: Fox, D., Gomes, C.P. (eds.) Proceedings of the Twenty-Third AAAI Conference on Artificial Intelligence (AAAI 2008), Chicago, 13–17 July 2008, pp. 1808–1809. AAAI Press (2008)
8. Kohavi, R., Becker, B.: Adult data set. https://archive.ics.uci.edu/ml/datasets/Adult. Accessed Feb 2017
9. Lafuente-Lechuga, M., Faura-Martínez, U.: Análisis de los individuos vulnerables a la exclusión social en españa en 2009. Anales de ASEPUMA **21**, 3003–3023 (2013)
10. Levitas, R., Pantazis, C., Fahmy, E., Gordon, D., Lloyd, E., Patsios, D.: The Multidimensional Analysis of Social Exclusion. Social Exclusion Task Force, Cabinet Office, London (2007)
11. Nwana, H.S.: Software agents: an overview. Knowl. Eng. Rev. **11**, 205–244 (1996)
12. Park, J.-E., Oh, K.-W.: Multi-agent systems for intelligent clustering. Int. J. Comput. Electr. Autom. Control Inf. Eng. **1**(11), 275–280 (2007)
13. Ponni, J., Shunmuganathan, K.L.: Multi-agent system for data classification from data mining using SVM. In: 2013 International Conference on Green Computing, Communication and Conservation of Energy (ICGCE), pp. 828–832, December 2013

14. Ramos, J., Varela, A.: Beyond the margins: analyzing social exclusion with a homeless client dataset. Soc. Work Soc. **14**(2) (2016). http://socwork.net/sws/article/view/27/73

15. Rank, M.R., Hirschl, T.A.: Calculate Your Economic Risk. New york times (2016)

16. Serrano, E., del Pozo-Jiménez, P., Suárez-Figueroa, M.C., González-Pachón, J., Bajo, J., Gómez-Pérez, A.: A multi-agent architecture for labeling data and generating prediction models in the field of social services. In: Bajo, J., et al. (eds.) PAAMS 2017. CCIS, vol. 722, pp. 177–184. Springer, Cham (2017). https://doi.org/10.1007/978-3-319-60285-1_15

17. Serrano, E., del Pozo-Jiménez, P., Suárez-Figueroa, M.C., González-Pachón, J., Bajo, J., Gómez-Pérez, A.: Predicting the risk of suffering chronic social exclusion with machine learning. In: Omatu, S., Rodríguez, S., Villarrubia, G., Faria, P., Sitek, P., Prieto, J. (eds.) DCAI 2017. AISC, vol. 620, pp. 132–139. Springer, Cham (2018). https://doi.org/10.1007/978-3-319-62410-5_16

18. Serrano, E., Rovatsos, M., Botía, J.A.: Data mining agent conversations: a qualitative approach to multiagent systems analysis. Inf. Sci. **230**, 132–146 (2013)

19. Suh, E., TiffanyVizard, P., AsgharBurchardt, T.: Quality of life in Europe: social inequalities. In: 3rd European Quality of Life Survey (2013)

20. Wooldridge, M.: An Introduction to MultiAgent Systems. Wiley, New York (2009)

Multi-agent Systems for Epidemiology: Example of an Agent-Based Simulation Platform for Schistosomiasis

Papa Alioune Cisse[1,2(✉)], Jean Marie Dembele[1,2], Moussa Lo[1,2,3], and Christophe Cambier[2]

[1] LANI, UFR SAT, Université Gaston Berger, BP 234 Saint-Louis, Sénégal
papaaliounecisse@yahoo.fr,
{jean-marie.dembele,moussa.lo}@ugb.edu.sn
[2] UMI 209 UMMISCO, Paris, France
christophe.cambier@ird.fr
[3] LIRIMA, M2EIPS, Saint-Louis, Sénégal

Abstract. In this paper, we show the convenience of multi-agent systems to help computational epidemiology come to the rescue of mathematical epidemiology for its practical limits on modeling and simulation of complex epidemiological phenomena. Herein, we propose as an example, an agent-based simulation platform for schistosomiasis (commonly known as Bilharzia, which is a parasitic disease found in tropical and subtropical areas and caused by a tapeworm called schistosome or bilharzias) that we have experimented with actual data of schistosomiasis in Niamey (Niger).

Keywords: Complex systems · Mathematical modeling · Multi-agents system · Agent-based modeling and simulation · Schistosomiasis · Computational epidemiology

1 Introduction

Epidemiological phenomena often involve a large number of entities - host, vector, pathogen, environment, etc. - that can interact and give rise to complex dynamics ranging over several spatiotemporal scales. These dynamics can have serious health consequences like the spread over large geographical areas and the contamination of a large number of persons. Epidemiological phenomena, because of their evolution that results from the elements interactions, can be described as complex systems. To efficiently study them, it is necessary to go through a process of modeling and simulation in order to produce prediction tools and define prevention and control policies.

For many infectious diseases including schistosomiasis, mathematical modeling has proved to be a valuable tool for predicting epidemic trends and designing control strategies. But, still, they suffer from some conceptual limitations.

In this paper we thus present multi-agent systems as a complementary approach to push the limits of mathematical approaches in modeling the spread of epidemics, offering an agent-based simulation platform for schistosomiasis. Schistosomiasis is a disease vector for which fresh water (pond, river, canal, etc.) constitutes a transfer

© Springer International Publishing AG 2017
S. Montagna et al. (Eds.): A2HC 2017/A-HEALTH 2017, LNAI 10685, pp. 131–153, 2017.
https://doi.org/10.1007/978-3-319-70887-4_8

medium of the pathogen, from the final host (individual) to the vector (mollusk) and vice-versa. It is a parasitic disease found in tropical and subtropical areas, the spread of which is closely related to the nature of water activity of populations in potentially infectious water points.

After presenting in Sect. 2 computational epidemiology by confronting it with mathematical epidemiology, we expose, in Sect. 3, the agent-based approach for modeling the spread of infectious diseases. Section 4 shows the relevant of agent-based approach for modeling schistosomiasis. In Sect. 5, we present the platform we propose for Schistosomiasis, experimentations, and simulations.

2   Computational Epidemiology

2.1   From New Epidemiological Challenges on the Spread of Diseases

Traditional mathematical epidemiology has always been an essential discipline for epidemiological problems and continues to be so. It focuses on the use of models based on differential equations to represent disease. These models, when combined with appropriate methods of analysis, may be appropriate tools for predicting future epidemics, comparing alternatives and methods, and can even help prepare effective intervention strategies of combatting the evolution of diseases [1, 2]. In these models, the population represented in the study of a disease is partitioned into subgroups according to various criteria (e.g.: the demographic characteristics and pathological states), and differential equations allow to describe the dynamics of the disease through these subgroups [3, 4]. However, it should be noted that most of mathematical epidemiology models to study the dynamics of disease, are based on ordinary differential equations (ODE). These models, neglecting the spatial aspect in the spread of disease, are based on the assumption that the population in question, with its various sub-groups (e.g.: Susceptible, Infected and Recovered) is distributed homogeneously on the space [4]. In the literature, this approach for modeling the spread of infectious diseases is sometimes highly criticized when the role of space is considered [1]. [5], through several examples, provide clear evidence that some infectious diseases spread geographically.

To overcome the problem of space in the ODEs models, other mathematical models, based on partial differential equations (PDE), are used to reject the homogeneous mixture of the population and represent the geographical spread of disease [6]. Yet, these models based on PDE, as well as those based on ODE, deal with subgroups of the population, represented in the equations, as *"continuous entities, and neglect the fact that populations are composed of individuals in interaction"* [4, 7]. This is problematic when we observe the social and interactional aspects of populations in the spread of disease. Indeed, these models do not take into account the complexity of human interactions which serve as a mechanism for the transmission of diseases [8].

Through different epidemiological concerns such as roles of geo-spatial, social and interactional aspects in the spread of disease, new epidemiological challenges of modeling and simulation are to examine to better understand and fight against the spread of infectious disease [1, 3, 9].

The challenge to make complex models of infectious diseases. It should be noted with [3], that the potential weakness of mathematical models is their inability to grasp the complexity inherent in the propagation of infectious diseases. Yet, this complexity is, in part, involved in human interactions and behavior which are apprehended through the networks of social and spatial (or geographical) interactions [8, 10]. It is for these reasons, for instance, that most recent surveys in epidemiology [1, 8, 10, 11], announce an urgent need for using computer science to develop models, for explaining the spatial, social, and interactional aspects to better understand the spread dynamics of infectious diseases.

The challenge of data integration in models. Data used in modeling and simulation are more and more stored in newer formats like Geographic Information System (GIS) [1]. Thus, as emphasized in [11], there is an urgent need to develop computational tools to take into account these data because, *"the integration of these data in simple compartmentalized epidemiological models is often difficult, requiring the use of computer models which are more complex, but also more effective"*.

Ultimately, computer epidemiology is a discipline the main objective of which is the application of computer concepts and resources (including technical, approaches and tools for modeling and simulation), and geographical tools (including tools for the representation and visualization of complex geospatial data) to provide epidemiologists with friendly tools which enable them to better understand the fundamental problems of epidemiology, such as the spread of disease.

2.2 To Computer Solutions for Modeling and Simulation

Considering the various considerations in the previous section, other computing paradigms of modeling and simulation can now be used in epidemiology: cellular automata and multi-agent systems [1, 10]. We focus here on the multi-agent systems because it is the most commonly used computer modeling approach in the literature.

3 The Agent-Based Modeling of Infectious Diseases

3.1 Agents and Multi-agents Systems

There are, in the literature, several perceptions, and thus definitions, of the concepts of agents, multi-agent system, environments, etc. In this section, we propose some which we judge helpful in modeling the spread of infectious diseases in general and the spread of schistosomiasis in particular. A multi-agent system is a dynamic system, and its dynamism usually comes from two factors: the behavior of agents and the dynamics of the environment [12]. We consider the environment here as composed of the physical (or spatial) and social milieu. The dynamics of the physical environment specifies the principles, processes and all the rules that govern and support the actions and interactions of agents [13]. The dynamics of the social environment, often determined as an organization (a set of roles, groups, etc.), specifies constraints that tell agents how they should behave [13, 14]. The agent behavior is usually specified by a perception-decision-action loop [15] (see Fig. 1). With this behavioral loop, agents are often seen as consisting of two parts: the body and the mind. The body serves as an interface to an agent, allowing them to perceive and act in the physical environment [16]; the spirit of an agent allows them to make decisions based on their perceptions of their internal state (representation of the world, memory, constraints of the social environment, …) [12].

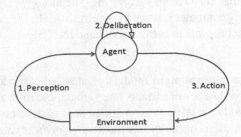

Fig. 1. Behavior of an agent (perception-decision-action loop) (source: [12])

In the description of the dynamic behavior of the agents, we deliberately distin-guished two processes performed by agents: a behavioral process (perception, reaction) that occurs in the physical environment and a decision-making process (deliberation, communication, etc.) involving the social environment. These are the two types of representations that exist in multi-agent systems: Reactive Architecture and cognitive architecture. There is an intermediate representation that combines the two architectures: it is the hybrid architecture [17–19]. In our work, we are more interested in hybrid architectures, especially those based on the principle of separation between the body and the mind of an agent [14, 20, 21]. The idea, as stated in [12], is to separate the decision-making mechanisms of the agent (internal dynamics): their mind, their action and perception mechanisms of the environment: their body. Thus, agents are present in two environments in which they perform different but complementary processes. The multi-agent system is seen as a two-level design system [17].

3.2 Agent-Based Multi-level Modeling

In an agent-based modeling and simulation approach, there are a number of constraints that must always be taken into account: the modeling objective, scientific theories, data and resources of calculation available [22]. These various constraints, among others, assigned to the modeling and simulation approach are sufficient to determine how the models are constituted. They allow identifying the parts or dynamics of the reference system to be represented, to choose the different agents (and possibly their levels of organization) to integrate into the model, to determine the level of description and simplification of these representations, to choose modeling and simulation techniques, etc. [22–24].

In this regard, choice of the agent's level of description and organization is decisive for the design of an agent-based model. In the classical approach of Multi-Agent Systems, there are essentially two representation's levels in models [24]:

- Microscopic level: it is the lowest level that corresponds to the description of the individual behaviors of the agents and their interactions.
- Macroscopic level: This is the highest level that corresponds to the emerging structures of the system. This is, for example, what is remarkable about the system by an external observer.

However, as shown in Fig. 2, only the microscopic level is represented in the model. The macroscopic level, emerging from agent interactions, corresponds to simulation outputs, and is not present in the model.

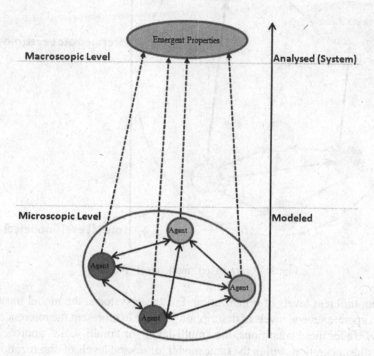

Fig. 2. Agent-based "mono-level" modeling

This approach, "*mono-level in design and bi-level in the analysis of emerging structures*", is sometimes not adapted for certain complex systems such as epidemiological phenomena which "*are often characterized by many heterogeneous entities of different dimensions, at different levels of organization, interacting in a complex way on very different scales of time and space*" [24]. For these systems, it is sometimes necessary to combine several points of view at different levels of abstraction; and/or several dynamics at different spatial-temporal scales. The justifications for this approach are many and varied. They may depend on constraints related to the modeled system itself, but also on constraints relative to the computing resources available for the simulations.

Indeed, it may happen that scientific theories that describe the reference system manipulate entities of different levels of abstraction and organization; or combine complementary dynamics of different space and time scales. Data available on the system to be modeled may also be of different types (quantitative or qualitative); and

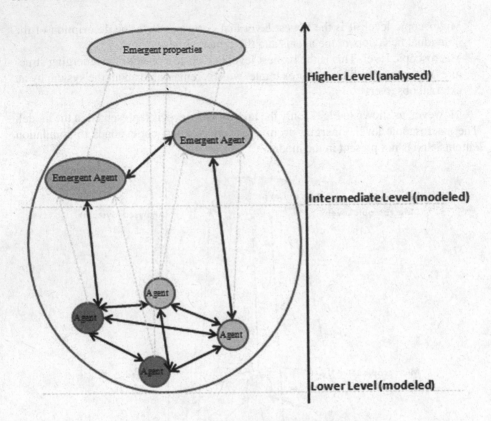

Fig. 3. Agent-based "multi-level" modeling

come from different levels of organization. For these systems, the model must necessarily incorporate several levels of description in order to represent the reference system faithfully. Under these conditions, the "multi-level" or "multi-scale" approach corresponds to the integration, within the same model, of several levels of organizations. This amounts to interacting organizations of agents operating on different time and space scales.

In the literature, some approaches propose to represent, in the design of a model, several agents' levels of descriptions: the microscopic level, which is the level of individual description of agents, and other levels, which may correspond to structures (emerging from the low level) that have an interactional meaning for the other agents. These emerging structures are reified into agents and exist as such in the model, as well as the low-level agents with which they can interact.

To ensure this, these models incorporate properties allowing them to detect dynamically emerging structures; to reify them as macroscopic agents; to represent the consequences of these reifications on the global system and to ensure the interactions of these emerging agents with the agents of low levels. For further details, the reader may refer to the following references: [23–27].

Moreover, other approaches propose to represent a multi-level system as a set of interacting models, where each model represents a level of description. This approach, which proceeds by "models coupling", corresponds sometimes to a combination of different complementary dynamics, intervening at different scales of time and space. See Sect. 5 for our example of models coupling.

3.3 Agent-Based Models of Infectious Diseases

Generally, modeling the spread of an infectious disease in a population with the agent-based approach is doubly beneficial. On the one hand, it allows to individualize populations (representing each individual as agent) in order to take into account their individual actions and interactions between them that are essential in the transmission of an infectious disease from one person to another. On the other hand, it helps integrate spatial and social dimensions which are specific to the spread of epidemics. In this regard, an agent-based model of the spread of an infectious disease is generally composed of [10, 28, 29]:

- A population of agents where each agent is described by two components: a set of identifiers attributes (including their health) and a set of behaviors that include their individual actions (e.g., moving from one place to another) and the actions they perform in relation with other agents (e.g., buy a product in direct contact with a seller).
- A space environment, which generally describes the objects in the environment used by agents (e.g., schools, markets, businesses, roads, water points, ...) and rules for using these objects (e.g., moving on a road in a very precise direction, undressing to swim in a pool, etc.).
- A social environment, which generally describes groups of agents (e.g., co-workers, classmates, members of a household, ...) and behavioral rules within these groups (for example, in a traditional village, boys are charged with fetching water from the river, by turn, for the needs of the household; women are responsible for doing the laundry and washing in the river, etc.).

In the literature, many recent studies use the agent-based approach to model the spread of infectious diseases. Here are, without details, few references on malaria [30, 31]; on tuberculosis [1]; on Rubella [10]; on influenza [28]; on Dengue [32]; on Fever Rift Valley [33].

4 Relevance of the Agent-Based Approach for Modeling Schistosomiasis

4.1 From a Multi-dynamic View of the Schistosomiasis Transmission

The life cycle of the pathogen responsible for schistosomiasis consists of two parts: intra-host dynamics and extra-host dynamics.

The intra-host dynamics gives the evolution of the parasite inside the organism of an individual (Human or Mollusk). In humans, it begins as soon as the schistosomulum penetrates the skin of the individual and continues as long as he is alive and not cured. In the mollusk (intermediate host), it begins with the penetration of the parasite in larval form called miracidia. This parasite's intra-host mechanism gives rise to interactions between several elements and results in the release of parasite's eggs through the urine or excreta of the final host; and the formation and release (by the intermediate host) of thousands of larvae called cercariae. This allows the pathogen to continue its evolution outside its hosts: it is the extra-host dynamics, called dynamics of transmission.

Moreover, the transmission dynamics, which ensures the passage of the parasite from one individual to another, is a complex phenomenon involving several heterogeneous entities of different natures and sizes, also operating in different environments.

We have subdivided this dynamics into two parts see Fig. 4): the infectious dynamics and the water access dynamics (we called it "social dynamics"). This social dynamics concerns the level of organization of the populations and is apprehended at the level of their physical and social environment. The infectious dynamics concern interactions in aquatic environments. We proposed to position this infectious dynamics (that happened on water) on the scale of the human space environment and we called it "spatial dynamics".

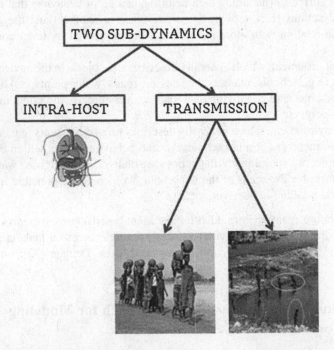

Fig. 4. Multi-dynamic view of the transmission of schsitosomiasis

The *spatial dynamics* of schistosomiasis refers to the role of the evolutionary environment of individuals (habitats), mollusks and larvae (the water points) in the transmission of the disease. Indeed, transmission of schistosomiasis can only be perpetuated if all the entities involved (final hosts, intermediate hosts, pathogens, etc.) converge in time and space in suitable water points (pond, river, Channel, etc.) [34]. This situation is justified by the fact that individuals environment of evolution is different to that of mollusks and larvae. Hence the relevance, on the one hand, of the "Human-water contact" problematic; and on the other hand, the frequencies, durations and intensities of human-water contacts which are closely related to the nature of the water points: characteristics relative to their accessibility (geographical distances with the dwellings) and the water activities they allow (bathing, linen, crockery, agriculture, etc.). It is for these reasons, among others, that we posed the problematic of the spatial dynamics of Schistosomiasis.

The *social dynamics* of schistosomiasis refers to the role of the social environment of populations in the activities they perform in water points. Indeed, for [35] and so many other authors, an understanding of who, where, how, when and why people engage in behavior which puts them at risk of perpetuating or contracting schistosomiasis through water contact activities should be an essential input in any integrated Schistosomiasis control programs. The answers to these questions must be sought in the time, space, social and cultural context of each studied population. It is in this context that we state the "Human-Water contact" problem. Thus, many work are interested in the identification of different types of water contact activities (essential occasions of Human-Water contacts), as well as socio-economic factors behind these activities. In [36], authors point the finger at the inefficiency of control strategies against schistosomiasis, often based on a classical approach of intermediate host's systemic control, combined with medical treatment of infected persons, which are established without any social concern of the populations concerned. Citing few cases where, despite control strategies, the disease stabilizes or returns after being defeated; they argue that continuous schistosomiasis reproduction cannot be understood, nor interrupted, by means of single biological approach, but should be understood in its socio-cultural context as a process capable of producing an epidemiological structure containing several determinant levels for its occurrence. So, social dynamics of schistosomiasis focuses on the Human-water contact patterns (types of water activities carried out in water, the nature of these activities, the classes of individuals performing these activities, the behavior of the populations during their contact activities, etc.); on social, economic, cultural, and religious conditions of populations and on possible links between the different elements of these two sets.

4.2   To a Multi-level System of Interactions

The multi-level aspect of the Schistosomiasis transmission phenomenon is dependent on its multi-dynamic aspect. These dynamics involve interactions that occur at very different scales: the intra-host scale and the extra-host scale. The entities involved in these two levels of interaction are also at different natures and sizes.

We can already consider intra-host dynamics as a level of interactions (the lowest level) encapsulated in entities (final and intermediate hosts) belonging to higher level of organization. The second level of interactions is that of transmission (in aquatic environment), involving the pathogen, the mollusk and the individual. We propose to isolate and then reposition this dynamics in aquatic environments in the organization's level of individuals (the highest level). Indeed, on the spatial scale, water points, constituting exclusively the mollusks environment of evolution, are integral parts of humans environment.

The Fig. 5 above shows three levels of interactions that we have identified in the Schistosomiasis transmission: social interactions level (highest level), aquatic interactions level (intermediate level), and intra-host interactions level (the lowest level).

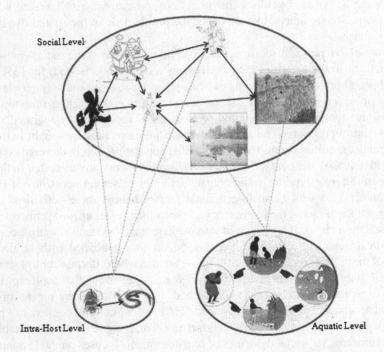

Fig. 5. Transmission of Schistosomiasis seen as a system of multi-level of interactions

From this point of view, modeling the phenomenon of schistosomiasis transmission would require an intra-host model (encapsulated in each host), an infection model for each water point and a model of the social organization of the population. In this work, we are particularly interested in the social organization's level. From the point of view of the dynamics underlying the transmission of Schistosomiasis, this level of organization represents both the "spatial dynamics" and the "social dynamics" of Schistosomiasis.

5 Our Agent-Based Simulation Platform for Spatial and Social Dynamics of Schistosomiasis

5.1 The Platform Backgrounds

In the study of social and natural complex phenomena, it is sometimes necessary to combine several dynamics or more views of a system to properly understand its operation and development [23, 37]. Thus, modelers of these systems are increasingly confronted with difficulties of representing them with a single model. Moreover, they are usually based on multi-disciplinary theories and use different modeling approaches to represent these systems. This often results, firstly, in the fact of having several models for a system, and secondly, in the need to properly integrate these different models to better understand the systems. It is in this context that our platform intervenes.

Indeed, in previous works [38, 39], we made separate studies of spatial and social dynamics of schistosomiasis, offering, respectively, two multi-agent models of these dynamics. However, these two models based on agents were established in two opposite directions for Multi-Agent Systems (cognitive and behavioral approach or reactive approach). In the study of social dynamics of schistosomiasis, the model based on agents that we have proposed, is based on cognitive architecture called BDI (Belief, Desire, Intention) to represent the mental processes of agents [38]. This model, without considering the behavior of the agents, deals exclusively with their decision and deliberative aspects. A platform dedicated to this type of representation was implemented and simulated in JASON [40]. In the study of the spatial dynamics, the established model focuses on behavioral aspects and reactive agents [39]. It is implemented with the GAMA platform [41].

From a global point of view, this system must be seen as a multi-agent model in which each agent, to decide how to behave in their environment (behavioral model), questioned their mental state, which is represented in a cognitive model as a separate decision engine: it is the separation principle of mind/body we dealt with above.

5.2   Basic Assumptions of the Platform

General case. Our platform fits in the context of the study of human-water contact activities (individuals' activities in potentially infectious water points). Specifically, it is interested in the following question: why do people continue to contaminate water during their excretory activities and contacting potentially infectious water sources? To answer this question, we consider water activities as part of a dynamic social process instead of a series of discrete activities performed by individuals [35].

Thus, water activities appear as a set of tasks that can be located in time and in space; and dependent on well-determined socio-economic conditions. Considering human activities as taking place only at specific locations and limited time periods, we make the distinction between the activities of an individual based on their degree of flexibility in time and space: the fixed activities (such as the fact of going to school) are those that cannot easily be reprogrammed or postponed; while flexible activities (such as swimming) can be so without difficulties [42, 43].

Let us consider the activity of "going to school" for a schoolboy. This activity, which is fixed, in so far as it is programmed a priori and constitutes an obligation for the student, takes place only in a specific location and within a period time well-defined. One can easily identify constraints linked to the execution of this activity: it only suffices that the current day be a school day, and the current time a school hour as well. On the other hand, an activity such as "swimming" in a pool or a canal is a flexible activity. Indeed, for a schoolboy, this activity may depend on several parameters: enough free time outside mandatory activities, availability and accessibility of a water site for this activity, a favorable temperature for practice, etc. In addition, unlike the fixed activities where, for a given period of time, only one activity is feasible; several flexible concurrent activities can be realized in the same period of time. The choice of either of them will depend on real-time constraints.

Indeed, on an off-day (e.g. Sunday), the schoolboy may want to carry out these activities in the day: "staying at home", "fetching water," "swimming with friends" etc. We cannot define a priori any order in the realization of these activities, or whether they actually will be realized. Nevertheless, we can define a set of constraints or criteria relating to the realization of each activity. We call these criteria "determining factors".

Case study. The specific case that is modeled and simulated with our platform is that of schoolboy in the city of Niamey. The data are expressed as variables that can provide vital information at multiple levels on the schoolboy's behavior:

- Local level: data are relative to some districts of Niamey city. They cover 23 districts which are socioeconomically and geographically characterized [44, 45]:
  - Socio-economically, there are three types of districts: Modern districts (modern housing, home water supply, low population density, upper social class); Renovated districts (modern or traditional housing, public standpipes, middle social class); Traditional districts (traditional housing, lack of water supply, high population density, disfavored social classes and migrants).
  - Geographically, there are three types of areas according to their location relative to the Niger River: waterside districts (the river is one of the boundaries of districts), central districts (which are limited by other districts) and peripheral districts (those with an open limit outside Niamey).
- Domestic level: data are relative to domestic household environments. They cover 900 households in the 23 districts, and relate to the type of habitat (precarious housing or villas), household water supply, household income, etc. [44].
- Individual level: data are relative to schoolboys themselves [44, 45]. They involve 1000 students belonging to the 900 households in the domestic level and are on their age, gender, houses (households, districts, and schools).

5.3 The Architecture of the Platform

From a conceptual point of view, we must see the architecture of the platform, as described in Fig. 6, as being composed of two levels of abstraction: a cognitive level and a behavioral level. It is a hybrid architecture in the sense of [17]. Each level of conception is managed by a platform dedicated to its type of representation: the cognitive level in JASON and the behavioral level in GAMA. Our platform therefore couples GAMA and JASON. In the interactions, the behavioral model (GAMA) transmits environmental characteristics to the decisional model (JASON) which, in turn, selects and transmits to the behavioral model the behavior that agents should take in the environment.

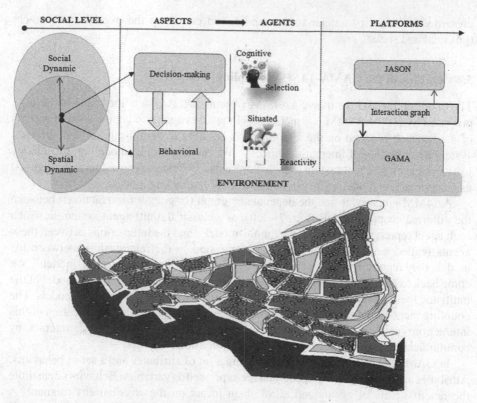

Fig. 6. (Above): Architecture of the platform. (Below): Visualization of the Niamey's GIS in GAMA with only districts (in gray), schools (in yellow), the Niger's River (blue) that affect our simulations; green elements represent schoolchildren. (Color figure online)

From a semantic and syntactic point of view, we must see that both models represent the same agents (and therefore have the same number of agents), but with different processes, according to different formalisms as well. The decisional model represents the agents' decision-making behavior (selection, deliberation, etc.) and social behavior (communication, negotiation, influence, etc.), while the behavioral model represents active and interactional behavior in the physical environment.

The decisional model defines a library of plans (representing all the activities that schoolboy can perform in the day) and a selection function, based on a process of multi-criteria decision, intended to select the appropriate action plans, under the real-time conditions of environment. For its part, the behavioral model implements the agents' activities on the physical environment. It also incorporates Niamey's geographic (housing, water environments, roads and their specific characteristics) and social configurations of populations. The latter aspect is specified in specific elements: districts and households (see previous section). All of these elements (houses, aquatic environments, roads, districts, schools, households and their specific characteristics) are incorporated into a Geographic Information System (GIS). The set of files that makes up GIS is presented as initial parameter to the model, and constitute the overall environment (physical and social).

5.4   Outline of the GAMA-JASON Coupling

The coupling method we use is AA4MM (Agents and Artifacts for Multi-Modeling), proposed by [12]. AA4MM is a meta-model that uses agents to couple a set of models of a system. It is based on the idea that it is possible to "multi-model" a multi-level system as "a society of interacting models". We must see multi-modeling, by analogy to a classical multi-agent system (which represents a system as a set of interacting agents) as an approach to modeling a system into a set of interacting models.

AA4MM proposes to see the dependency graph (or graph of interactions) between the different coupled models (Fig. 7 - left), as a classical multi-agent system in which each agent represents a model of the "multi-model", and the interactions between these agents (called model agents or m_{agents}) correspond to the relationships between the models they represent (Fig. 7 - right). Thus, from "a society of interacting models", we come back to a system of interacting agents, where each agent represents a model of the multi and their interactions represent the relations between their respective models. The coupling meta-model proposed by AA4MM therefore relies on the specification of this interactions environment between these "m_{agents}". In AA4MM, m_{agents} interact by communicating asynchronously using **communications artifacts**.

In GAMA, an agent is given by specifying a set of attributes and a set of behaviors. Attributes are used to identify agents and are expressed as variables. Behaviors constitute the reactive parts of agents and allow them to act on the physical environment. A behavior is expressed by specifying the word "reflex" (to say that the behavior is

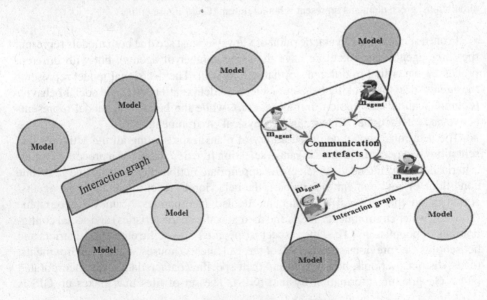

Fig. 7. Multi-modeling in AA4MM

automatically executed at each simulation step, if its execution condition is verified), followed by the name of the behavior, its execution condition (optional) and the body of the behavior which is a sequence of basic actions performed by the simulator: *reflex nom_comportement when: condition {corps}*.

Table 1. Agents of the behavioral model: their attributes and some behaviors

AGENTS	ATTRIBUTS	BEHAVIORS
Global	- current_day (int) - current_hour (int)	- *init( )* ; Initializes the parameters of the model by loading the GIS files of Niamey's ; It creates at the same time the other agents. - reflex *loadDecisionsFromJason { }* ;
Schoolboy	- **sexe (string)** - **decision (string)** = { *'goToSchool', 'stayAtSchool', 'goHome', 'stayAtHome', 'goToWater', 'playInWater', 'fetchWater'* } - **situation (string)** = { *'goingSchool', 'atSchool', 'goingHome', 'atHome', 'goingToWater', 'playingInWater', 'fetchingWater'* } - **myQuarter (Quarter)** - **myHousehold (HouseHold)** - **mySchool (School)**	- *reflex goToSchool when : decision=' goToSchool' { }*; - *reflex stayAtSchool when : decision='stayAtSchool'{ }*; - *reflex goHome when : decision='goHome' { }*; - *reflex stayAtHome when : decision='stayAtHome' { }* ; - *reflex goToWater when : decision='goToWater' { }*; - *reflex playTime when : decision='playTime' { }*;
LastAgent		- *reflex sendDataToJason { }* ;

Table 1 gives an overview of *Global*, *Schoolboy* and *LastAgent* agents of our GAMA model. The two agents *Global* and *LastAgent* form together the $m_{agent}AC$ (Fig. 8: above) which represents the behavioral model in the multi-model. Indeed, each agent of the GAMA model runs once in the same simulation step, according to the order given in Fig. 8-bottom:

(1) The Global agent runs first. This allows it, with its behavior *loadDecisionsFrom-Jason { }*, to load from the *D-C coupling artifact*, decisions made by agents (in JASON's model) and pass them to the relevant *Schoolboy* agents (ie agents for whom a new decision is made). To do this, it modifies (for each *Schoolboy* agent concerned) the *decision* attribute (String) with the new value loaded.

(2) It is based on the value of its *decision (string)* attribute, modified by the Global agent, that a Schoolboy agent performs a behavior. For example, if the value of the *decision* (string) attribute of a *Schoolboy* agent is *'goToSchool'*, it executes its *goToSchool { }* behavior, which is supposed to move it from its place to its school.

(3) Finally, it is the *LastAgent* agent that runs the last one. Its unique behavior (*sendDataToJason { }*) is to inquire about the situation of each Schoolboy agent (where it is, what it is doing, its social conditions), environmental data (eg, Attributes *current_day (int)* and *current_hour (int)* of the Global agent, representing respectively the current day and the current time), etc., and to send all this information to

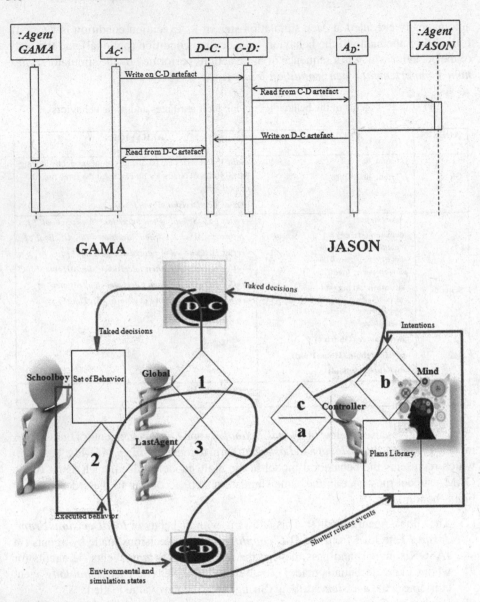

Fig. 8. GAMA-JASON coupling model

the **C-D coupling artifact**. These data are intended to the m_{agent} **AD** representing the decisional model in JASON.

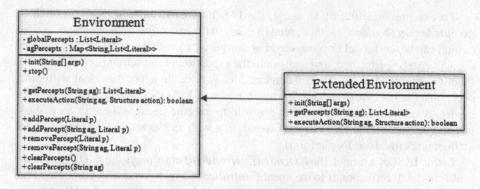

Fig. 9. Extension and customization of the JASON environment (From [46])

The JAOSN platform offers a special framework for programming a multi-agent system in which agents, in addition to their deliberative architectures (which enable them to produce actions), can share knowledge; objectives; know-how, propose services, coordinate their actions, etc. [46]. JASON also provides support to implement a virtual environment model where agents are located and can execute the actions generated in the decision-making processes. This virtual environment is implemented in JASON with a JAVA class (called *Environment*) capable of executing agent's actions.

This *Environment* class (extensible and customizable) provides a set of functions allowing agents to operate on their *execution environment* and to perceive the properties and consequences of actions they produce. It thus acts as a link between the decision-making aspects of JASON agents (their decision-making architectures) and their dynamic and reactive aspects (Fig. 10).

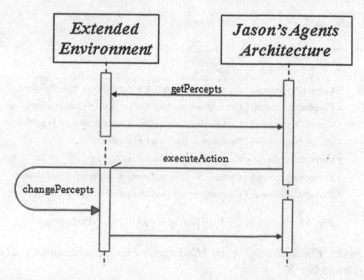

Fig. 10. Interactions between the execution environment and the decision-making architecture of a JASON agent (From [46])

To execute an action of an agent, the JASON's **Environment** class, through its **executeAction (boolean)** method, sends a query to the *execution environment* of actions (which can be any model implemented For this purpose) with the name of the agent and the action to be performed; and waits until the execution of the action is completed (the function returns true) to inform the agent. Meanwhile, the agent may deal with other decisions. For our case, the *execution environment* of JASON's agents is the behavioral model of GAMA. In this way, it is possible to execute agent actions in an isolated environment (the GAMA platform), separately with the execution of their internal architectures (the JASON platform).

In this JASON's model, the **ExtendedEnvironment** class plays the A-D m_{agent} in the multi-model. It corresponds to the agent **Controller** of Fig. 8-bottom. A part of the Plan Library that defines the JASON's schoolboy agents (corresponding to the **Mind** agents in Fig. 8-bottom) is given in the following Fig. 11.

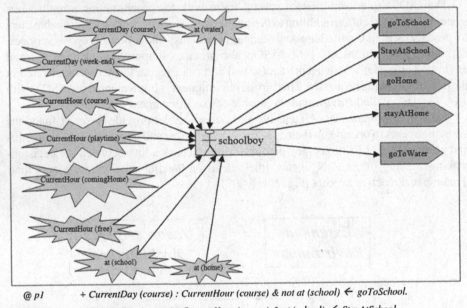

@ p1	+ CurrentDay (course) : CurrentHour (course) & not at (school) ← goToSchool.
@ p2	+ CurrentDay (course) : CurrentHour (course) & at (school) ← StayAtSchool.
@ p3	+ CurrentDay (course) : CurrentHour (comingDown) & not at (home) ← goHome.
@ p4	+ CurrentDay (course) : CurrentHour (playtime) ← StayInSchool.
@ p5	+ CurrentDay (course) : CurrentHour (playtime) ← goToWater.
@ p6	+ CurrentDay (course) : CurrentHour (comingDown) & at (home) ← goToWater.
@ p7	+ CurrentDay (course) : CurrentHour (comingDown) & at (home) ← StayAtHome.

Fig. 11. A part of the Plan library for JASON's Mind agents

In our model, **Controller** agent and **Mind** agents execute continuously according to the order given in Fig. 8:

(a) Using its *getPercepts (String ag): List <Literal>* behavior (Fig. 9), the *Controller* agent loads from the *C-D coupling artifact*, data (about agents and their environ- ment) from the behavioral model and passes them to *Mind* agents as trigger events of actions plans.

(b) It is according to the perceived events that a *Mind* agent executes its internal archi- tecture in order to decide on the behavior to be held (production of an action to be executed in the execution environment).

(c) With its *executeAction (String ag, Structure action): Boolean* action, the *Controller* agent performs the action taken by a *Mind* agent, passing it to its corre- sponding agent in behavioral model through the *D-C coupling artifact*.

5.5 Experimental Settings of the Platform

With the platform, we aim to reproduce, by simulations, the rates of daily use of the banks of the Niger River by schoolchildren (rates provided by survey data in [45]). The basic idea is to lean on the socio-economic conditions of schoolchildren (the determining factors), expressed in the decisional model in the form of explanatory variables, to determine the schoolboys' behavior related to their access to the river banks. For this, we have defined a set of variables that are used as "determining factors" to determine the susceptibility of a schoolboy to frequent waters: age, gender, type of habitat (relative to their family living standards), the water supply of their home (how their family gets water: whether they use water from the river for household needs), the type of district (social class, human density in the district), the geographical location of their home vis- à-vis the River of Niger (the distance between their home and the river), their free time (leisure time spent to perform water activities in the river banks). In the experiment of the platform, all these variables are frozen (because from survey data), except the free time. It is the only model parameter to be calibrated to reproduce the "schoolboy-river" contact rate expected. It represents the free time available for the schoolboy when they can perform their water activities for a whole day.

The execution step of the platform is 5 min (the time a schoolboy needs to walk to school, for example). Thus, "free times" of schoolchildren to carry out their water activ- ities are precisely determined in the simulations: break time: usually, between 10 a.m. and 11 a.m., on working days; rest time: ordinarily, between 1 o'clock p.m. and 3 o'clock p.m. for the day, then between 5 and 7 p.m. for the afternoon. Actually, this is the moment between the very time when the student gets home after the end of classes (which is relative to the walked distance to get home) and the next school time (3 or 7 p.m.); all the morning and all the evening, on off-days (Saturday and Sunday). In all these situa- tions, the only flexible activities (apart from the other fixed activities) that we take into account in our simulations for each schoolboy are: (@P1) going to the water during free time; or (@P2) staying at home (for resting time) or at school (during the break). For each of these two flexible activities (@P1 and @P2), all the factors (or explanatory variables) that determine their choice are to be specified in the model. These variables are then used by the selection function to determine the eligibility of each activity (by calculating an eligibility value that can be positive, zero or negative) and choose the activity that has the greatest value of eligibility. For (@P2), no factor has been defined in the model, to determine its choice: its eligibility is therefore always zero for all schoolboys. For (@P1), the determining factors are: (during rest): distance between the schoolboy's school and the river; and duration of break time; (during break and off-days): in short all the factors defined above. Thus, (@P2) is chosen only when the eligibility of (@P1) is negative.

5.6   Simulations of the Platform

The objective of the simulations is to see how the free time of schoolchildren, added to other influencing factors, influences their susceptibility to go to water during days of class. For this, we choose as an indicator, the daily rate of "schoolboy-river" contact provided by survey data in [45]; and reproduced in [39]: This contact rate turns around 20.5%, on working days. In the first scenario, each schoolboy uses their default free time that is:

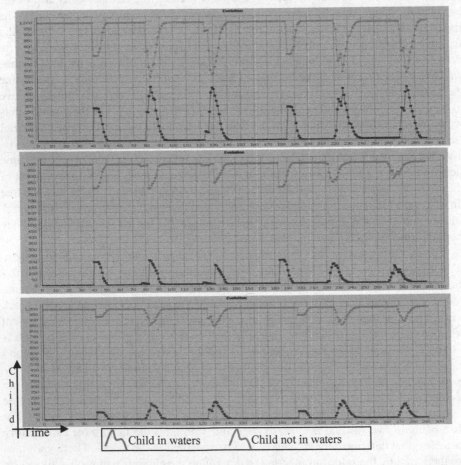

Fig. 12.   (Up) "school-river" contact rate with default unoccupied time: ~45%. (Middle) "school-river" contact rate with default unoccupied time – 30 min: ~20%. (Down) "school-river" contact rate with default unoccupied time – 45 min: ~17%.

60 min (during breaks); and 60 to 115 min, the time of the following class (i.e., 3 p.m. or 7 p.m.) - the time to come home after the end of class (i.e., 1 p.m or 5 p.m.). Simulations of outputs are given in Fig. 3 (up).

In other scenarios, we try the experiment which consists in finding the ideal free time to meet the expected contact rate (~20.5%). For this, we gradually diminish the schoolboys' free time. In the second scenario, we have decreased by 30 min the free time of each schoolboy. Simulations outputs are given in Fig. 3 (Middle). Finally, in a third scenario, we reduced by 45 min the free time of each schoolboy. Simulations outputs are given in Fig. 3 (down).

Comparing these three scenarios (Fig. 3) with the daily use of the river by schoolchildren which is 20.5% during working days [39, 45], the ideal free time (Scenario 3 - Fig. 3 (Middle)) is that during which schoolboy is still busy at least 30 min during resting moments and break times (Fig. 12).

6   Conclusion

In this paper, we presented computational epidemiology as a complementary approach to deal with some epidemiological aspects (spatial and social aspects in particular) on the spread of infectious diseases, aspects for which epidemiological mathematic (especially Equations-based models) have limits. From this point of view, we focused on the relevance of agent-based approach to model and simulate schistosomiasis and its dynamics of spread.

The model presented (which is a coupling of spatial and social dynamics of the disease) and experimented by co-simulation of GAMA and JASON, where are implemented respectively a behavioral model of the spatial dynamic and a decision-making model of the social dynamic, clearly shows its predictive and explicative capacities. It allows reproducing the rate of utilization of the Niger River's banks by Niamey's child and explaining the influence of children's leisure time on their exposure to the risk of contracting schistosomiasis.

References

1. Patlolla, P., Gunupudi, V., Mikler, A.R., Jacob, R.T.: Agent-based simulation tools in computational epidemiology. In: Böhme, T., Larios Rosillo, V.M., Unger, H., Unger, H. (eds.) IICS 2004. LNCS, vol. 3473, pp. 212–223. Springer, Heidelberg (2006). https://doi.org/10.1007/11553762_21

2. Bonabeau, E., Toubiana, L., Flahault, A.: Evidence for global mixing in real influenza epidemics. J. Phys. Math. Gen. **31**(19), L361 (1998)

3. Marathe, M., Ramakrishnan, N.: Recent advances in computational epidemiology. IEEE Intell. Syst. **28**(4), 96–101 (2013)

4. Fuks, H., Lawniczak, A.T.: Individual-based lattice model for spatial spread of epidemics. Discrete Dyn. Nat. Soc. **6**(3), 191–200 (2001)

5. Fukś, H., Duchesne, R., Lawniczak, A.T.: Spatial correlations in SIR epidemic models, mai 2005. arXiv:nlin/0505044

6. Murray, J.D., Stanley, E.A., Brown, D.L.: On the spatial spread of rabies among foxes. Proc. R. Soc. Lond. B Biol. Sci. **229**(1255), 111–150 (1986)

7. Fu, S.C., Milne, G.: A flexible automata model for disease simulation. In: Sloot, P.M.A., Chopard, B., Hoekstra, A.G. (eds.) ACRI 2004. LNCS, vol. 3305, pp. 642–649. Springer, Heidelberg (2004). https://doi.org/10.1007/978-3-540-30479-1_66

8. Barrett, C.L., Eubank, S., Marathe, M.V.: An interaction-based approach to computational epidemiology. In: AAAI, pp. 1590–1593 (2008)

9. Gorder, P.F.: Computational epidemiology. Comput. Sci. Eng. 12(1), 4–6 (2010)

10. Perez, L., Dragicevic, S.: An agent-based approach for modeling dynamics of contagious disease spread. Int. J. Health Geogr. 8, 50 (2009)

11. O'Hare, A., Lycett, S.J., Doherty, T., Salvador, L.C.M., Kao, R.R.: Broadwick: a framework for computational epidemiology. BMC Bioinform. 17, 65 (2016)

12. Siebert, J.: Approche multi-agent pour la multi-modélisation et le couplage de simulations. Application à l'étude des influences entre le fonctionnement des réseaux ambiants et le comportement de leurs utilisateurs. Ph.D. thesis, Université Henri Poincaré - Nancy I (2011)

13. Weyns, D., Omicini, A., Odell, J.: Environment as a first class abstraction in multiagent systems. Auton. Agents Multi-agent Syst. 14(1), 5–30 (2007)

14. Stratulat, T., Ferber, J., Tranier, J.: MASQ: towards an integral approach to interaction. In: Proceedings of the 8th International Conference on Autonomous Agents and Multiagent Systems, vol. 2, pp. 813–820 (2009)

15. Ferber, J.: Les systèmes multi-agents: un aperçu général. Tech. Sci. Inform. 16(8) (1997)

16. Demange, J.: Un modèle d'environnement pour la simulation multiniveau - Application à la simulation de foules. Ph.D. thesis, Université de Technologie de Belfort-Montbeliard (2012)

17. Muller, J.P.: Des systemes autonomes aux systemes multi-agents: Interaction, emergence et systemes complexes, HDR, Habilitation a diriger des recherches – Informatique (2002)

18. Jennings, N.R., Sycara, K., Wooldridge, M.: A roadmap of agent research and development. Auton. Agents Multi-Agent Syst. 1(1), 7–38 (1998)

19. Chaib-Draa, B., Jarras, I., Moulin, B.: Systèmes multi-agents: principes généraux et applications. Ed. Hermès, pp. 1030–1044 (2001)

20. Payet, D., Courdier, R., Sebastien, N., Ralambondrainy, T.: Environment as support for simplification, reuse and integration of processes in spatial MAS. In: 2006 IEEE International Conference on Information Reuse and Integration, pp. 127–131 (2006)

21. Boissier, O., Bordini, R.H., Hübner, J.F., Ricci, A., Santi, A.: Multi-agent oriented programming with JaCaMo. Sci. Comput. Program. 78(6), 747–761 (2013)

22. Treuil, J.-P., Drogoul, A., Zucker, J.-D.: Modélisation et simulation à base d'agents: exemples commentés, outils informatiques et questions théoriques. Dunod: IRD, Paris (2008)

23. Gaud, N.A.: Systèmes multi–agents holoniques: de l'analyse à l'implantation: méta-modèle, méthodologie, et simulation multi-niveaux. Besançon (2007)

24. Gil-Quijano, J., Hutzler, G., Louail, T.: De la cellule biologique à la cellule urbaine: retour sur trois expériences de modélisation multi-échelles à base d'agents. In: 17ème Journées Francophones sur les Systèmes Multi-Agents (JFSMA 2009), Lyon, France, pp. 187–198 (2009)

25. Servat, D., Perrier, E., Treuil, J.-P., Drogoul, A.: When agents emerge from agents: introducing multi-scale viewpoints in multi-agent simulations. In: Sichman, J.S., Conte, R., Gilbert, N. (eds.) MABS 1998. LNCS, vol. 1534, pp. 183–198. Springer, Heidelberg (1998). https://doi.org/10.1007/10692956_13

26. Maquerlot, F., et al.: Dual role for plasminogen activator inhibitor type 1 as soluble and as matricellular regulator of epithelial alveolar cell wound healing. Am. J. Pathol. 169(5), 1624–1632 (2006)

27. Dembele, J.M., Cambier, C.: An agent-particle model for taxis-based aggregation; emergence and detection of structures. Procedia Comput. Sci. 9, 1484–1493 (2012)

28. Khalil, K.M., Abdel-Aziz, M., Nazmy, T.T., Salem, A.B.M.: An agent-based modeling for pandemic influenza in Egypt. In: Lu, J., Jain, L.C., Zhang, G. (eds.) Handbook on Decision Making. Intelligent Systems Reference Library, vol. 33, pp. 205–218. Springer, Heidelberg (2012). https://doi.org/10.1007/978-3-642-25755-1_11

29. Shi, Z.Z., Wu, C.-H., Ben-Arieh, D.: Agent-based model: a surging tool to simulate infectious diseases in the immune system. Open J. Model. Simul. 2(1), 12–22 (2014)

30. Reyes, A.M., Diaz, H., Olarte, A.: An agent-based model for the control of malaria using genetically modified vectors. In: ECMS, pp. 31–36 (2012)

31. Ferrer, J., Albuquerque, J., Prats, C., López, D., Valls, J.: Agent-based models in malaria elimination strategy design. In: EMCSR 2012 (2012)

32. Daudé, É., Vaguet, A., Paul, R.: La dengue, maladie complexe. Nat. Sci. Sociétés 23(4), 331–342 (2015)

33. Paul, P.N.T., Bah, A., Ndiaye, P.I., Ndione, J.A.: An agent-based model for studying the impact of herd mobility on the spread of vector-borne diseases: the case of rift valley fever (Ferlo Senegal). Open J. Model. Simul. 2(3), 97–111 (2014)

34. Kloos, H., Gazzinelli, A., Van Zuyle, P.: Microgeographical patterns of schistosomiasis and water contact behavior; examples from Africa and Brazil. Mem. Inst. Oswaldo Cruz 93(Suppl 1), 37–50 (1998)

35. Watts, S., Khallaayoune, K., Bensefia, R., Laamrani, H., Gryseels, B.: The study of human behavior and schistosomiasis transmission in an irrigated area in Morocco. Soc. Sci. Med. 1982 46(6), 755–765 (1998)

36. Barbosa, C.S.: Epidemiology and anthropology: an integrated approach dealing with bio-socio-cultural aspects as strategy for the control of endemic diseases. Mem. Inst. Oswaldo Cruz 93(Suppl 1), 59–62 (1998)

37. Fianyo, Y.E.: Couplage de modèles à l'aide d'agents: le système OSIRIS, Paris 9 (2001)

38. Cisse, P.A., Dembele, J.M., Lo, M., Cambier, C.: Assessing the spatial impact on an agent-based modeling of epidemic control: case of schistosomiasis. In: Glass, K., Colbaugh, R., Ormerod, P., Tsao, J. (eds.) Complex 2012. LNICSSITE, vol. 126, pp. 58–69. Springer, Cham (2013). https://doi.org/10.1007/978-3-319-03473-7_6

39. Cisse, P.A., Dembele, J.M., Cambier, C., Lo, M.: Multi-agent simulation of water contact's patterns in relation to schistosomiasis: a BDI architecture using kernel functions. In: 2014 Second World Conference on Complex Systems (WCCS), pp. 536–541 (2014)

40. Bordini, R.H., Hübner, J.F., Wooldridge, M.: Programming Multi-agent Systems in AgentSpeak Using Jason. Wiley Series in Agent Technology. Wiley, Chichester (2007)

41. Drogoul, A., et al.: GAMA: a spatially explicit, multi-level, agent-based modeling and simulation platform. In: Demazeau, Y., Ishida, T., Corchado, J.M., Bajo, J. (eds.) PAAMS 2013. LNCS, vol. 7879, pp. 271–274. Springer, Heidelberg (2013). https://doi.org/10.1007/978-3-642-38073-0_25

42. Hägerstrand, T.: What about people in regional science? Pap. Reg. Sci. Assoc. 24(1), 6–21 (1970)

43. Miller, H.J.: A measurement theory for time geography. Geogr. Anal. 37(1), 17–45 (2005)

44. Ernould, J.-C., Labbo, R., Chippaux, J.-P.: Evolution de la schistosomose urinaire à Niamey. Niger. Bull. Société Pathol. Exot. 96(3), 173–177 (2003)

45. Ernould, J.C., Kaman Kaman, A., Labbo, R., Couret, D., Chippaux, J.P.: Recent urban growth and urinary schistosomiasis in Niamey, Niger. Trop. Med. Int. Health 5(6), 431–437 (2000)

46. Bordini, R.H., Bazzan, A.L.C., Jannone, R. de O., Basso, D.M., Vicari, R.M., Lesser, V.R.: AgentSpeak(XL): efficient intention selection in BDI agents via decision-theoretic task scheduling. In: Proceedings of the First International Joint Conference on Autonomous Agents and Multiagent Systems: Part 3, New York, pp. 1294–1302 (2002)

Author Index